Cherokee Nation v. Georgia
Native American Rights

Victoria Sherrow

Landmark Supreme Court Cases

Enslow Publishers, Inc.

40 Industrial Road   PO Box 38
Box 398   Aldershot
Berkeley Heights, NJ 07922   Hants GU12 6BP
USA   UK
http://www.enslow.com

Library of Congress Cataloging-in-Publication Data

Sherrow, Victoria.
    Cherokee Nation v. Georgia: Native American rights / Victoria Sherrow.
        p. cm. — (Landmark Supreme Court cases)
    Includes bibliographical references and index.
    Summary: Discusses the cases brought by the Cherokee Nation and its supporters
against the state of Georgia beginning in the 1830s to protect the rights of the Cherokee
living there.
    ISBN 0-89490-856-1
    1. Cherokee Indians—Trials, litigation, etc.—Juvenile literature. 2. Georgia—Trials,
litigation, etc.—Juvenile literature. 3. Cherokee Indians— Georgia—Legal status, laws,
etc.—Juvenile literature. [1. Cherokee Indians—Trials, litigation, etc. 2. Cherokee
Indians—Legal status, laws, etc. 3. Indians of North America—Georgia—Legal status,
laws, etc.] I. Title II. Series.
    KF228.C4594S53   1997
    346.75801'3—dc21   96-39651
                                            CIP
                                            AC

Printed in the United States of America

10 9 8 7 6 5 4 3

Photo Credits: Cherokee Nations Communications, pp. 20, 110; Library of
Congress, pp. 7, 12, 16, 39, 69, 82; National Archives of Canada, p. 102;
Smithsonian, pp. 35, 94, 97; Supreme Court Archives, pp. 44, 62, 72.

Cover Illustrations: *Trail of Tears* courtesy of Woolaroc Museum, Bartlesville, OK
(inset); Franz Jantzen "Collection of the Supreme Court of the United States"
(background).

Contents

1

In Search of Justice

In 1830, a group of Cherokee leaders went to Washington, D.C., the capital of the United States. They were there to present a petition to government officials. The petition was signed by thousands of Cherokees and it listed the grave problems that faced these people.

The Cherokee leaders hoped that Congress would defeat a bill that was being debated in the House of Representatives and the Senate. The bill sought to remove the Cherokee people from their homes in the southeastern states and move them to lands west of the Mississippi River. Through previous treaties, the Cherokee people had already given up most of their ancestral lands. In one treaty, the United States government had promised that they could keep the rest of their land, except what they gave up or sold of their own free will.

To make matters worse, most of the Cherokees, now living in Georgia, were being subjected to harsh state laws. The Cherokee council explained how these laws were "suspended in a most terrifying manner over a large part of our population."[1]

The federal government had long dealt with the Cherokee people as a separate nation, but the state of Georgia refused to do so. It said that the Cherokee people had no right to organize their own government. They could not make their own laws or rule themselves within the state's boundaries. Georgia was trying to control many aspects of Cherokee life. The state was denying the Cherokee people basic human rights. These rights, however, were guaranteed under the Constitution of the United States.

The Cherokee people considered Georgia's actions both immoral and illegal. These actions violated treaties between the Cherokee people and the United States. The United States government had pledged to protect them from this type of state interference. Yet President Andrew Jackson had said he would not take action against Georgia. The petition said, "It would be impossible to describe the sorrow which affected our minds, on learning that [President Jackson] had come to this

Andrew Jackson was President of the United States when the Cherokee leaders brought their petition to Washington, D.C. Though the Cherokee people had treaties with the United States, Jackson would not aid them in their claims against the state of Georgia.

conclusion. . . ."[2] The Cherokee people said that, by ignoring Georgia's actions, the government would "leave our people to the mercy of the neighboring whites, whose supposed interests would be promoted by our expulsion or extermination."[3] This was by no means the first time Cherokee leaders had appealed to United States government officials. It would also not be the last. Their struggle would eventually lead them to the United States Supreme Court.

An Ancient Homeland

By the 1830s, the Cherokee fight for justice had been going on for decades. Whites had first arrived on Cherokee lands in the 1500s. Since then, the Cherokee Nation had struggled to survive as a people in the face of sweeping changes.

The Cherokee people are one of the oldest groups to inhabit North America. They were among five Native American groups in the southeastern United States that whites called the Five Civilized Tribes. Through the centuries, the Cherokee people had developed a way of life that worked well for them. It was based on their understanding of nature and the relationships among living things and the spiritual world.

White explorers arrived in the region in 1540. At this time, about twenty-five thousand Cherokees lived in some two hundred villages throughout the present-day states of Virginia, Tennessee, Georgia, Alabama, and North and South Carolina. Their lands included dense forests, hills and valleys, and streams and rivers where they fished for food. Deer, bear, and other game roamed the woods. The Cherokee people raised corn, beans, squash, and other crops in the rich soil.

More newcomers arrived after the late 1600s. By 1673, white men, often from colonies set up in Virginia, were coming to trade beads, cloth, ribbons, and guns for deerskins. The years that followed brought many problems. First one group of Europeans claimed Cherokee lands. Then other groups arrived and pushed the Native Americans out. The newcomers also brought unfamiliar diseases. Thousands of Native Americans died from them.

Still, the Cherokee people tried to get along with the newcomers. During the 1700s, people traveling in the Southeast were impressed by the hospitality, manners, and attractive communities of the Cherokee people. But as more settlers gravitated to the pleasant climate and beauty of Cherokee country, conflicts increased.

The Cherokee people made numerous adjustments as white settlers flooded their lands. The settlers brought very different attitudes and ways of life. Some white men married Cherokee women. This could disrupt communities if the white men moved their families away or abandoned their wives and children.

A String of Treaties

In 1785, the Cherokee people signed their first treaty with the new United States. It guaranteed their right to live on their homelands. It was the first of many treaties that were later broken. Like other Native Americans, the Cherokee people began to doubt whether they could depend on such agreements.

During their many negotiations with whites, Cherokees spoke eloquently about their rights. During the 1785 meeting, Corn Tassel, a respected elder statesman, told United States commissioners:

> It is a little surprising that when we entered into treaties with our brothers, the whites, their whole cry is *more land!* . . . Suppose in considering the nature of your claim . . . I were to ask one of you, my brother warriors, under what kind of authority, by what law, or on what pretense he makes this exorbitant demand of nearly all the lands we hold between your settlements and our towns. . . .[4]

Corn Tassel argued that battles won did not give whites the right to claim Native American lands. If that were true, he pointed out, Cherokees could march onto lands where whites lived and declare that land conquered. He then said:

Let us examine the facts of your present eruption into our country, and we shall discover your pretensions on that ground. What did you do? You marched into our territories with a superior force; our vigilance gave us no timely notice of your maneuvers; your numbers far exceeded us, and we fled to the stronghold of our extensive woods, there to secure our women and children. . . . Your laws extend not into our country, nor ever did.[5]

In 1791, Cherokee leaders signed a new treaty with the United States government. They surrendered large areas of land. In exchange, they got a promise that they would keep what was left of their land forever. Later, white citizens demanded more Cherokee land, and the government broke its promise. In the decades that followed, Native Americans were forced to give up more and more land. Cherokee leaders wondered: How much land is enough for the whites? When will they leave us alone?

A Separate People

As they became familiar with white culture, the Cherokee people adapted some things for their own use. For example, the white man's "talking papers"—letters and books—inspired them to develop a Cherokee alphabet and written language. This system was completed by 1819. It enabled the Cherokee people to read and write in their own language. Some Cherokees also changed to the Christian religion.

The Cherokee people adopted portions of the white man's culture. For example, Sequoyah invented an eighty-six character alphabet so that his people could start recording their history.

In general, however, Cherokees did not think their ways were inferior to those of the whites. They did not believe they should be forced to change. Many agreed with Corn Tassel, who said in his famous 1785 speech:

> . . . many proposals have been made to us to adopt your laws, your religion, your manners and your customs. But we confess that we do not yet see the [reasons we should make such changes.] . . .[6]

Corn Tassel said that his people would prefer to see white people behave in ways that showed they had high moral standards and respect for others. He also said that his people could just as well ask why white people did not live as his Native Americans did. He said, "The great God of Nature has placed us in different situations. It is true that he has endowed you with many superior advantages; but he has not created us to be your slaves. *We are a separate people!*"[7]

By the 1800s, the Cherokee were primarily a farming people. They were not really considered warriors and hunters. They lived much like their white neighbors, with an organized government and education system. Cherokee leaders traveled regularly to Washington. They worked out agreements and spoke to members of Congress about their situation. They hoped that, from time to time, United States laws would protect them and the government would honor its treaties.

In various southeastern states, however, laws were designed to force the Cherokee people out. Settlers attacked Cherokee villages and moved further onto Cherokee lands. Year after year, treaties and promises were broken. The laws, which seemed to change regularly, did not protect the Cherokee people. White leaders often changed their mind and broke their word. Native American leaders did not know whom they could trust or whether the white man's law would ever treat them fairly.

Wide-Ranging Issues

The Cherokee people struggled for their rights in the Southeast. Native Americans throughout the continent, however, also faced serious problems during the 1800s. The debate over Native American rights began soon after whites first settled in North America. It reached a crisis as the Cherokee people sought help from the Supreme Court during the 1830s.

The issues embodied in those cases affected the whole nation, not just Native Americans. These issues were discussed by political leaders, in the press, at churches, at public meetings, and by citizens in every region. Many white Americans supported the Cherokee cause. Journalists wrote articles in their favor. Members of Congress and other public figures spoke out on their behalf.

Cherokee leaders knew that white Americans could turn to the United States Supreme Court with legal disputes that could not be settled elsewhere. Now, with their future at stake, they, too, turned to the white man's Court. Misled and mistreated, the Cherokee people placed their hope in the law. Perhaps this highest of all courts would resolve the matters of Native American rights that threatened so many people.

The Cherokee people would seek help from the United States Supreme Court not once but twice, in 1831 and 1832. These lawsuits were known together as the Cherokee Cases. They brought the problems of Native Americans squarely before the American legal system. They forced the new United States to examine some complex moral and legal questions: What was the legal status of Native Americans? Who actually owned the land? Who had authority over Native Americans? How should treaties between the federal government and tribes be negotiated? How should the resulting agreements be handled at the state level?

The results of the Cherokee Cases would be far-reaching. They affected relations between Native

Chief Justice John Marshall was a Supreme Court Justice from 1801 to 1835. He would write the decisions for both of the Cherokee Cases.

Americans and the United States government for more than a century. Historian Wilcomb E. Washburn later wrote: "On his [Chief Justice John Marshall's] decision, hinged the title to the real estate of the nation, the independence of numerous Indian nations, the sanctity of treaty rights, and even the very existence of law and order."[8]

2

A Clash of Cultures

The problems that led to the Cherokee Cases of the 1830s actually began centuries before. Cultures clashed as the Cherokee people and other Native Americans tried to live alongside newcomers to the newly forming United States. The ways of life, cultures, and religions of the newcomers were quite different from those of the Cherokee people. Native Americans and whites often found themselves at cross purposes. Native Americans hoped to stay in their homelands. White settlers, however, wanted these lands for themselves. States wanted to expand and govern, free from the presence of Native American communities or tribal laws and governments. Unfortunately, the Native Americans who lived on the lands before the white settlers ever arrived were now stuck in the middle.

Whites in the Southeast

The Cherokee people probably first encountered whites in 1540. This is when Spanish explorer Hernando de Soto came to the region. De Soto, with his large group of soldiers, slaves, and horses, was searching for gold. Instead, the Spaniards found farms and villages. De Soto and his people were angry and scornful of the Native Americans. They murdered hundreds of them.

Other white settlers followed. They brought health hazards to the Native Americans. The Native Americans had never been exposed to smallpox, measles, typhoid fever, and other contagious diseases that were well-known in Europe. They lacked immunity (physical resistance) against these diseases and had no effective treatments. Before the 1500s, there were about twenty-five thousand Cherokees. By 1700, as a result of disease and killing, there were about sixteen thousand left.[1]

During the 1700s, English settlers arrived in the Southeast. These settlers were fairly peaceful. They began trading metal tools and other goods for deerskins. They sent the deerskins to Europe to be made into clothing, mostly men's breeches, a type of pants. The English also exchanged their goods for prisoners of war captured by the Native Americans. They sold these prisoners to white landowners as slaves. The slave trade declined after 1750. The deerskin trade

The Cherokee people first came into contact with whites in 1540, and continue to live in the United States today. Shown here is former Principal Chief Wilma Mankiller and a group of schoolchildren.

thrived, however, leading to a drop in the deer population. The Native Americans gave up some of their old ways of doing things once metal tools were available. That, and the declining number of deer, made them more dependent on trade with the white settlers.

Who Owns the Land?

European leaders were aware that the Western Hemisphere was rich in land and other resources. They sent financed expeditions to what they called the new world. North America, however, was already inhabited by hundreds of thousands of Native Americans. This raised important moral and legal issues about who really owned the land. According to widely accepted political views of the day, white men could settle on and take possession of any land they found in North America. This created problems for the Native Americans, who firmly believed that they were entitled to inhabit the land of their ancestors.

How did Europeans justify their actions? One line of reasoning was called the doctrine of discovery. Under this rationale, the first European to discover an area of land in North or South America could claim it for his country. That country would hold title to the land in the eyes of international law. Native Americans who occupied the land were said to have aboriginal title. It was a lesser standing that gave Native Americans few rights. It also subjected them to the laws of those European countries that claimed the land.

Most Europeans came to the Americas with little or no interest in understanding the native cultures. To further defend taking the land, Europeans defined Native Americans as "savages." Whites claimed they roamed about and were not qualified to hold any legal titles. They also said that Native Americans followed the "wrong"—non-Christian—religions. Using these arguments, they could say that it was God's will that Christian Europeans take over.[2] Some people also argued that America was vast and mostly empty. Why not let people come and take portions they needed for their settlements?

Some Europeans disagreed with these ideas. There were intense debates about Native American rights. During the 1550s, a Spanish philosopher named Sepúlveda argued that it was right to take Native American lands. Bartóleme de Las Casas, another Spanish philosopher, said it was wrong. Franciscus de Victoria, a Spanish judge, said that since Native Americans owned the land before Spaniards came to the Americas, no "discovery" could take place. He contended that no religious or royal leader had the right to divide up lands in North America and give them to others. How could a king grant something he did not possess? asked de Victoria.

While these debates went on an ocean away, settlers from Europe continued to come to the Southeast. Different countries vied for power. The Cherokee people and other tribes sometimes took sides and became involved in the newcomers' disputes over who should govern.

Relations With the English

The Cherokee people tried to adjust to their new situation. They first befriended the English settlers. In 1730, a chief named Moytoy was given the title "emperor" by Sir Alexander Cuming, an English explorer. Moytoy accepted the title and pledged loyalty to the English. He sent King George II a fur crown decorated with eagles' tails.

That year, seven Cherokee men visited King George II in England. They dined lavishly, received gifts of fine clothing, and had their portraits painted. The Cherokees were impressed with the fine buildings, ships, and businesses they saw in London. When they returned home, they urged their fellow Cherokees to stay on good terms with the English and trade with them exclusively.

Between 1754 and 1763, England and France fought a series of battles called the French-Indian Wars over land in North America. The English pledged to protect the Cherokee people from their enemies if they would fight with English troops in the Ohio Valley. Native Americans who supported the French included the large, powerful Iroquois, who lived mostly in the northeastern United States, and the Choctaw.

However, during the 1750s, the Cherokee-English alliance broke down and bloody confrontations took place. Cherokee villages were destroyed and thousands died, either during battles with white settlers or from illness or starvation. After the English defeated the French, they demanded that the Cherokee people give up a large tract of good hunting land. This caused more problems for the Native Americans.

The Cherokees were relieved when the English king issued the Proclamation of 1763. It banned any settlement west of the Appalachian Mountains. This meant that Cherokee hunting lands in what is now northeastern Tennessee would be secure. However, their relief was short-lived, because American settlers ignored the king's edict.

A Bloody Revolution

When England fought against rebellious American colonists during the Revolutionary War, the Cherokee people sided with the English. They resented the way

American settlers had moved onto their land. They believed that the English might treat them better.

During 1776, Cherokee warriors attacked several southern colonies, killing American settlers. American soldiers attacked Cherokee villages, killing men and women. They also took Cherokee children to sell as slaves. In one raid in South Carolina during the summer of 1776, American soldiers destroyed thousands of bushels of stored corn. Many Cherokees starved during the winter that followed. Other Cherokee towns and food stores and livestock were destroyed during the war. Some Native Americans escaped to the area of western Tennessee and hid in the mountains to wait for the war to end.

"Peace and Friendship"

After the Revolutionary War ended in 1783, the Cherokee people adjusted to more changes as the newly formed United States government took shape. The years between 1776 and 1794 were troublesome and confusing. The Cherokee people had already given up some twenty thousand square miles of land. The United States government told them that their remaining lands were now located within the boundaries of "states." These states were inhabited by white settlers. They also had different leaders and different laws with which the Cherokee people must deal.

On November 28, 1785, the Cherokee people signed their first formal agreement with the United States. The Treaty of Hopewell said that the United States Congress would give peace to all of the Cherokees. It would receive them into "the favor and protection of the United States of America."[3] The boundaries of Cherokee land were defined, and the treaty said that any United States citizen or other non-native who tried to settle there or on Cherokee hunting grounds "shall forfeit the protection of the United States, and the Indians may punish him, or not, as they please."[4] Article 13 of the treaty declared: "The hatchet shall be forever buried, and the peace given by the United States, and friendship re-established between the United States on the one part, and all the Cherokees on the other, shall be universal. . . ."[5]

In 1791, another treaty called the Treaty of Holston was accepted by Cherokee leaders and ratified by President George Washington and Congress. This treaty stated the intention of the parties to establish "permanent peace and friendship." It defined the boundaries of Cherokee land "for all time" and granted the Cherokee people supplies and farming tools to promote agriculture since their hunting grounds were reduced.[6]

The Cherokee people hoped that the end of the war and their treaties with the United States would bring peace and stability. But assaults on their land and way of life continued.

Difficult Adjustments

United States political leaders and other whites suggested ways to "civilize" Native Americans. They thought that if Native Americans adopted white ways, they would be happier and more secure. In 1796, President Washington wrote to the Cherokee people. He said that "the game with which your woods once abounded, are growing scarce."[7] Washington and others advised the Cherokee people to rely more heavily on farming, adding wheat and cotton crops, and raising hogs, cattle, and sheep.

Government agents brought farm tools and seeds to Cherokee villages. This required more adjustments by the Native Americans. Before this time, women had traditionally done most of the farming. Now the men would have to get more involved. Also, the Cherokee people viewed their lands as belonging to the tribe, not to individuals. They did not understand how the white men in the United States government could think that the land belonged to them.

Missionaries came to Cherokee lands. They wanted to teach the Native Americans the English language and convert them to Christian religions. Some Cherokees did become Christians; others did not. Still others added certain Christian ideas to their own spiritual views.

For the Cherokees living in Georgia, the loss of land continued. Between 1802 and 1822, their holdings shrank from 26 million acres to 9 million. Georgians wanted more land for settlement and to grow cotton, a crop that was in great demand.[8]

In 1802, the United States government and Georgia made an agreement that would affect the Cherokee people profoundly. Georgia gave up its claim to nearby western lands, which then became the new states of Alabama and Mississippi. In return, the government pledged to "extinguish in Georgia's favor the Indian title of all lands within the boundaries of the state."[9] This meant that the United States government had promised Georgia it would one day have possession of land that now belonged to the Cherokee people. The federal government pledged to acquire Indian lands as soon as it could be done "peaceably" and on "reasonable terms."[10] Georgia made plans to give away these lands through a lottery system. That further increased public demand for the land.

Despite various treaties, most United States government officials wanted all eastern tribes to move west. This was a concept called removal. In 1803, through the Louisiana Purchase, France sold the United States its claim to lands west of the Mississippi River. These lands totaled more than 800,000 square miles. They stretched from present-day North Dakota to Louisiana. President Thomas Jefferson suggested that eastern tribes be given some of this land for resettlement. In the West, said Jefferson, Native Americans would be more free to live as they chose.

Some Cherokees became so concerned about their future in the Southeast that they accepted an offer by the United States government to move west. Between 1808 and 1810, a few thousand Cherokees migrated to land in the Louisiana Territory. But most remained in the Southeast. Many operated businesses and improved their farms and homes.

During these years, throughout the country, Native American land was taken in different ways: by purchase, by force, by treaty, or when white people settled on it and refused to leave. Sometimes Native American leaders were bribed and coerced into giving up tribal land.

Those Cherokees who remained in the Southeast

hoped that their treaties would enable them to live in peace. They helped the new United States during the War of 1812. Five hundred Cherokee warriors joined Andrew Jackson's troops to fight Creeks at the Battle of Horseshoe Bend. At one point, Chief Junaluska saved Jackson from being stabbed to death. Junaluska also figured out a clever way to attack the Creeks. This led to an American victory.

A New Cherokee Government

The Cherokee people wanted to protect their property and business holdings as well as their land. They also wanted a more unified government, one that would not allow leaders to negotiate on their own or for small groups of Cherokees.

To achieve these goals, the Cherokee people abandoned their centuries-old clan system of government. They chose instead one that resembled that of the United States. The lower house of the legislature, the National Council, consisted of four delegates elected from each of the eight districts in the Nation. The National Council elected twelve people to serve in the upper house, called the Standing Committee. (It was later renamed the National Committee.) The committee chose the three top Cherokee leaders: principal chief, assistant principal chief, and treasurer. It was empowered to make laws and approve treaties.

Losing Ground

In 1816, Assistant Principal Chief John Ross served on a Cherokee delegation that went to Washington, D.C. The delegation went to discuss the tribe's grievances with the government. Ross, the son of a white settler named Daniel Ross and a part-Cherokee mother, spoke English fluently. He had attended a mostly white academy in Kingston, Tennessee, and become a successful businessman. He was familiar with the world of whites as well as that of Native Americans. Ross had also fought in the Battle of Horseshoe Bend. His wife, Quatie, was a full-blood Cherokee.

Two years later, as president of the National Committee, Ross went to Washington again. He helped to negotiate terms for the Treaty of 1819. The treaty required the Cherokee people to give up thousands of acres in North Carolina, Tennessee, and Alabama— more than one-fourth of their remaining lands. This left them 10 million acres, compared to the 40 million acres they had occupied before 1540. Chief Pathkiller called their remaining land "this last little."[11] The United States government pledged that this land would belong to the Cherokee people *forever*, safe from intruders or other treaty-makers. Yet, as Cherokee leaders pointed out, the previous twenty-four treaties had been broken. Two-thirds of the Cherokee people now lived within the state of Georgia. They felt insecure, knowing that the United States had pledged in 1802 to terminate Native American claims to land inside Georgia's borders.

In 1819, the new Cherokee governing council held its first meeting, in Newtown, located in present-day Georgia near the union of the Coosawattee and Conasauga rivers. The council declared that the tribe would not sell or give up any more land. Any Cherokee who did so could be put to death. They also formed the Cherokee Light Horse (or Light Horse Guard) to expel trespassers.

The next year, President James Monroe asked Congress for money that he could offer those Cherokees still living in Georgia in exchange for their land. The United States government then asked the Cherokee council to negotiate terms for the removal of the remaining Cherokees.

By that time, some council leaders had visited the three thousand Cherokees who now lived out West. They were suffering from sicknesses and wars that were taking place among various tribes in the region. A Cherokee delegation replied to the government, "It is the fixed and unalterable determination of this nation never again to cede one foot more of our land."[12] They told President Monroe that the Cherokee people were "not foreigners, but the original inhabitants of America, and that they now stand on the soil of their own territory, and they can not recognize the sovereignty of any State within the limits of their territory."[13]

Confusing Years

The Cherokee people continued to strengthen their institutions. In 1825, Newtown, Georgia became the official capital of the Cherokee Nation and was renamed New Echota. Designed by Cherokee surveyors, New Echota included a town square flanked by government buildings—the Council House, Cherokee Supreme Court, and a printing office. By 1830, the capital housed several stores and a ferry. When the council was in session, the many social events attracted hundreds of visitors.

In 1824, Secretary of War John C. Calhoun created a Bureau of Indian Affairs under the Department of War. The bureau officials and men it appointed as "Indian agents"—white officials sent to teach Native Americans white ways—were authorized to enforce the law. People who committed crimes against Native Americans were arrested. However, many offenders were turned over to local law enforcement officials, who often did nothing. Many Native Americans considered the bureau useless in handling disputes that arose within the states.

The Cherokee people continued working with lawmakers in Washington. They sent delegations in 1824 and 1825. They met with Calhoun and the head of the Bureau of Indian Affairs, Thomas L. McKenney. Cherokee delegates were discouraged when Calhoun and McKenney would not give them a clear reading of certain treaties that had been made in the past. The officials also refused to remove an Indian agent whom the Cherokee people disliked.

In 1827, the Cherokee Nation wrote and approved a constitution. The document said that the tribe would not seek to expand its territory but that it fully intended to keep what it already owned. That same year, John Ross was elected principal chief.

The first issue of a weekly newspaper, the *Cherokee Phoenix*, came out on February 21, 1828. The *Phoenix* published many articles discussing the pros and cons of removal. A group called the Treaty Party, led by Stand Watie and the Ridge brothers, wanted the tribe to negotiate terms for a peaceful move to the West. These Cherokees thought it was hopeless to fight the United States government and its armies. That year, a group of

In 1827, John Ross was elected to be principal chief of the Cherokee Nation. Ross, who was part white and part Cherokee, knew English well, which allowed him to communicate easily with the United States government.

Cherokees did go west to found a community in present-day Arkansas and Texas. However, most Cherokees, led by John Ross, opposed removal.

By the late 1820s, the Cherokee people were living much like their white neighbors. About 93 percent were farmers. The average farm measured about eleven acres. They lived in small log homes, some with stables, smokehouses, and corn cribs for crops. Wealthier Cherokees owned plantations, sometimes staffed by slaves. Others operated stores and trading posts. They had a written language, an organized government, and a constitution. They believed their government and way of life were equal to that of whites. They had abided by treaty agreements and hoped to peacefully coexist with their neighbors. But their plans were to be dashed again.

3

Seeking Help From the Courts

Pressure on the Cherokee people to leave the Southeast mounted as Georgians sought access to the Tennessee River. By connecting their state with the Ohio and Mississippi rivers, they could transport cotton and other crops to new markets. Wilson Lumpkin, a congressman who would later become governor of Georgia, was among those who wanted to build railroads through Cherokee lands. They would run from southern Georgia to rivers in the North and West. Other events soon spurred the state to seek complete control of Cherokee lands.

To complicate matters, during the early 1800s, people were still arguing fiercely about states' rights versus federal powers and about the proper role of the United States Supreme Court. These conflicts made it all the harder for Native Americans to negotiate with the people in power and to rely on their promises. Tensions between the Cherokee people and whites increased even more during the summer of 1829. Gold was discovered in the southwestern part of "Cherokee country"—the land still legally owned by the tribe. The news spread, and gold seekers (prospectors) from other states joined Georgians who were also searching the hills for this precious metal. The Cherokee people refused to sell this land to Georgia. They ordered the prospectors and settlers to leave. Most prospectors found no gold. Some took Cherokee land, livestock, and other goods.

States' Rights vs. Federal Powers

The United States government had recognized Native American tribes as nations and negotiated with them through treaties. Because of this, states could not legally force tribes to sell land. Officials in Georgia, however, passed laws that would nullify (void) any laws passed by the Cherokee Nation. Georgia's laws ignored treaties between the Cherokee Nation and federal government. Like some other states, Georgia was testing the limits of its powers in relation to the federal government. This was part of an ongoing debate about states' rights versus

Wilson Lumpkin was among the people who wanted to build a railroad line through Cherokee lands. Lumpkin later became governor of Georgia.

federal authority. Many heated arguments arose in the United States Congress over what the states were legally allowed to do on their own. Many of these matters would not be settled for more than a century.

Numerous treaties supported the Cherokees' position. The Cherokee people hoped that President Andrew Jackson, elected in 1829, would force Georgia to honor those agreements. But Jackson's inaugural address disturbed them. He said he would give "humane and considerate attention to [the rights of Indians]" as was "consistent with the habits of our Government and the feelings of our people."[1] This was not good news for the Cherokee people.

In April 1829, Secretary of War John Eaton met with the Cherokee people to discuss Jackson's position. Eaton told them they could not live as an independent nation within Georgia. He also said that President Jackson would not interfere with how the states made their laws. In his annual message to Congress on December 8, Jackson pledged to support laws removing all Native Americans to the West. Historian Joseph C. Burke concludes, "The choice seemed simple to Eaton and Jackson. The Indians must move or submit to Georgia law. The President thought removal offered the only practical solution."[2]

Georgia passed new laws to make life more difficult

for the Cherokee people. Finally, facing a situation with no apparent solution, Cherokee leaders turned to the American legal system.

Confusing Legal Options

The United States Supreme Court had first ruled on a case involving Native American rights in 1810. The case, *Fletcher* v. *Peck*, was also called the *Yazoo* land case. In his opinion for the Court, Chief Justice John Marshall declared that Georgia could legally grant Native American land within its borders to land companies. Yet the Native Americans would still retain ownership of those lands. This opinion left many people confused.

Another important case reached the United States Supreme Court in 1823. Once again Chief Justice Marshall wrote the majority opinion. The case, *Johnson and Graham's Lessee* v. *McIntosh*, is often called the first of three Cherokee cases to reach the high court. The Court ruled that, under the federal Constitution, Native Americans were not independent nations with sovereignty (a free, independent status). In reaching its decision, the Court reasoned that "Indian rights to sovereignty, as independent nations" were diminished because discovery by Europeans of the land gave them exclusive title. This meant that

Europeans had control over the land in exchange for bringing European civilization and the Christian religion to the Native Americans.

In explaining his opinion, Marshall discussed the doctrine of discovery. He cited "the original fundamental principle that discovery gave exclusive title to those who made it."[3] Marshall said that from the early days of colonization to the present, the founders of the United States had supported this doctrine and it had become "the law of the land."[4]

Marshall showed how it had been politically convenient for American colonists to accept this doctrine. Somewhat ironically, he said, "The potentates of the old world found no difficulty in convincing themselves that they made ample compensation to the inhabitants of the new by bestowing on them civilization and Christianity."[5] Afterward, said Marshall, European rulers had left the discoverers and natives to sort out their own relationship, which led to the present confusion. He commented:

> While the different nations of Europe respected the rights of the natives, as occupants, they asserted the ultimate dominion to be in themselves; and claimed and exercised, as a consequence of this ultimate dominion, a power to grant the soil, while yet in possession of the natives.[6]

The *Johnson* decision showed that the United States

Supreme Court was not sure how to define the status of Native Americans. Marshall had said that, in some ways, they were dependent. Yet, in other ways, they were a distinct people occupying land that had first been claimed by England, then by the United States.

As for John Marshall, the Chief Justice found himself becoming more and more concerned about the way Native Americans were being treated. In 1828, he wrote a letter to his fellow Justice, Joseph Story, saying, "The conduct of our Fore Fathers in expelling the original occupants of the soil grew out of so many mixed motives. . . ." Marshall conceded that fear of Native American warriors had once sparked persecution of the tribes, but he said,

> . . . every oppression now exercised on a helpless people depending on our [generosity] and justice for the preservation of their existence, impresses a deep stain on the American character. I often think of indignation of our disreputable conduct—as I think it is—in the affair of the Creeks of Georgia, and I look with some alarm on the course now pursuing in the northwest.[7]

The Removal Act

On May 28, 1830, Congress passed the Indian Removal Act by a slim margin. The vote in the Senate was 28 to 19, while in the House, the bill passed by only five votes—102 to 97. This act empowered the president to

Joseph Story was one of the Supreme Court Justices who heard the Cherokee Cases. In 1828, prior to the trials, Story received a letter from Justice Marshall in which Marshall expressed regret over how the Native Americans had been treated by the United States.

divide land west of the Mississippi River into a number of districts "for the reception of such tribes or nations of Indians as may choose to exchange the lands where they now reside, and remove there...."[8] This meant that lands in the Southwest had now been officially set aside for Native Americans currently living in the Southeast. They were urged to relocate there. Congress budgeted $500,000 for the removal (relocation) process. Native Americans who agreed to move would be paid for their land and any improvements. The president was also authorized to promise tribes that their western lands would belong to them as long as they chose. He could take measures to protect the tribes on their new lands.[9]

President Jackson announced that he would meet that summer with leaders of the southeastern tribes. They would discuss the removal process. Principal Chief John Ross called for a General Council meeting in July. The council asked attorney William Wirt and Christian Missionary Jeremiah Evarts for advice. Under the assumed name William Penn, Evarts had opposed removal and had written many essays about the problems of Native Americans. His essays appeared in a magazine called the *National Intelligencer*. They had aroused sympathy for the Cherokee people. In the end, the council voted not to attend the meeting with President Jackson.

In a speech that December, Jackson praised the Indian Removal Act. He claimed that for progress to occur in civilization, sometimes one group of people had to make way for others. Jackson said the money being offered to the tribes for their land was "a fair exchange." Native Americans, he said, would be moving to a place that could improve their chances for survival.[10] He asked, "Can it be cruel in this Government . . . to purchase [the Native American's] lands, to give him a new and extensive territory, to pay the expense of his removal, and support him a year in his new abode?"[11]

A Heated Debate

Georgia resolved that all Cherokees must leave. State officials laughed at the Cherokee Constitution and its claims regarding the Native Americans' territory. The officials found support for their position in the 1823 *Johnson* case and President Jackson's speeches. Federal officials would not hinder their attempts to get rid of the Cherokee people and other southeastern tribes.

Jackson and others supported removal. Many political leaders and citizens, however, opposed it. They criticized Georgia's treatment of the Cherokee people and other tribes. Georgia officials resented people from other regions telling them how to deal with the tribes inside their state. They argued that other states would not tolerate having a separate nation of people living within state borders but operating under separate laws.

In June 1830, Georgia passed a bill saying that its state laws applied to everyone, including the Cherokee people. The Cherokee government had no legal standing. That December, Georgia lawmakers announced that large portions of Cherokee country would now become parts of various counties in Georgia. Furthermore, Georgia officials declared it illegal to form "a state within a state." They banned Cherokee political or council meetings in Georgia. Cherokees were forbidden to dig for gold on their own lands. Most alarming to the tribe was a law that barred Native Americans from testifying against any white person in Georgia courts.[12]

Troops called the Georgia Guard were formed to arrest any Cherokees who broke state laws or seemed to threaten Georgians. Guard members patrolled Cherokee lands on foot or on horseback. In return, they received fifteen to twenty dollars a month in pay. Under Georgia law, the Guard could:

> . . . arrest any person legally charged with or detected in, a violation of the laws of this State, and to convey as soon as practicable, the person so arrested before a Justice of the Peace, Judge of the Superior or Justice of Inferior Court, of this State, to be dealt with according to law. . . .[13]

47

Prominent whites, including some Georgians, criticized these laws. Senator Edward Everett of Vermont protested that the new laws permitted white men to commit crimes against the Cherokee people without fear of punishment. Everett said that:

> They may burn the dwelling, waste the farm, plunder the property, assault the person, murder the children of the Cherokee subject in Georgia, and though hundreds of the tribe may be looking on, there is not one of them that can be permitted to bear witness against the spoiler.[14]

Everett was equally blunt about the Removal Act, which he called "unmitigated evil." He told Congress that removal "cannot come to good. It cannot, as it professes, elevate the Indians. It must and will depress, dishearten, and crush them."[15]

The Cherokees were bitterly disappointed when their old "friend" Andrew Jackson failed to speak or act against these harsh new laws. Jackson claimed that he had "no power to protect them against the laws of Georgia."[16]

To make matters worse, the tribe faced financial problems. In a previous treaty, the United States had promised to pay them six thousand dollars a year. This had always gone directly to the Cherokee council. Under the new plan, payments were to be made directly to individual Cherokees. That meant giving each person about fifty cents, with some having to travel more than one hundred miles to collect this small sum. Many would never claim their money, nor could the council collect the unpaid funds to use for the benefit of the group.

Profound Cherokee Legal Questions

The Cherokee people ignored the law that banned meetings in Georgia. They held their October council at New Echota. The next month, a delegation met with officials in Washington, D.C. Northern journalists interviewed Cherokee leaders John Ridge, William Shorey Coodey, and Richard Taylor. Calvin Colton, a writer for the *New York Observer*, said the men were:

> . . . polished in their manners, and worthy of our society. . . . They enforce respect and esteem. . . . They actually know more of the institutions, laws, and government of the United States than a large fraction of those who occupy seats in the House of Representatives.[17]

Ridge gave members of Congress a five-page document. It listed Cherokee complaints about their treatment by white settlers, the Georgia Guard, federal Indian agents, and squatters, people who settled on the land illegally and refused to move. Among the prominent lawmakers who supported them in Congress were Davy Crockett, his fellow representatives from

Kentucky, and Senator Theodore Frelinghuysen of New Jersey.

The Cherokee delegation then met with Secretary of War Eaton. John Ridge asked Eaton what the federal government would do if Georgia tried to force the Native Americans out against their will. Eaton said the government would decide what to do if and when such a situation arose. The Cherokee people found this response vague and troubling.

With no support from the president or other top United States officials, where could the Cherokee people turn? Principal Chief John Ross and other leaders decided to seek legal help. This help was paid for by Ross and other wealthier tribe members. In 1830, they hired the Georgia law firm of Underwood and Harris and the Baltimore law firm of William Wirt. The attorneys in these firms believed in the Cherokee cause.

Wirt, originally from Virginia, was an expert on Native American legal matters. He had read records of numerous Congressional debates on the status of Native Americans and their lands. He was an attorney general under presidents James Monroe and John Quincy Adams. He had twice issued opinions that said the Cherokee people were an independent nation. In an 1830 letter, he said he was "struck with the manifest determination, both of the President and the State, that the State laws should be extended over [the Cherokees]. . . ."[18]

With their attorneys, the Cherokees tried to determine their rights under the law. There was little mention of Native Americans in the Constitution of the United States. As a result, the federal government had been forced to make decisions about the status of tribes and their lands in the years after it was written. The Cherokees and their attorneys concluded that the tribe needed a case that would eventually reach the United States Supreme Court. They must find a case that would force the Court to deal with Native American rights. It was only a few months before a case involving these issues arose.

A Legal Challenge

With the Georgia Guard policing Cherokee lands, there were bound to be confrontations. In September 1830, the Guard arrested Cherokee Corn Tassel (sometimes referred to as "George Tassels" or "George Corn Tassel" in court papers) for killing another Cherokee within Cherokee territory. The state of Georgia claimed authority in the matter. It tried Tassel at Hall County Superior Court. He was convicted and sentenced to death by hanging.

The Cherokee people denounced the trial and

verdict. The tribal council claimed that Cherokee laws, not those of Georgia, applied within the tribe's territory. Corn Tassel's attorney appealed the case to a Georgia superior court, asking it to overturn the conviction.

In the case of *The State of Georgia* v. *George Tassels*, the judges at the Georgia superior court level ruled that a state does have criminal and civil authority over tribes and their members who live within that state's boundaries. They said that it was not possible for a sovereign nation to exist if it held title to the land only by occupancy and not with a legal title as defined by American property law. Furthermore, the judges said Native Americans lacked the skill and intellect needed to handle their affairs properly and needed guidance from the federal government.

After this ruling in Georgia's favor, the Cherokees resolved to appeal the decision all the way to the United States Supreme Court. William Wirt agreed to represent the Cherokee people. He knew he might be harshly criticized by those who supported Georgia, including President Jackson. The case would also pose a big dilemma for the Supreme Court. Nonetheless, Wirt took it on. He wrote to James Madison, "I have a higher bar to answer at than any in this world, and if I can secure a judgment there, I care little for what the unworthy may say of me here."[19]

John Sergeant, another lawyer, also joined the case. Sergeant had served as chief counsel for the Bank of the United States. In August, Wirt and Sergeant filed an appeal asking the Supreme Court to issue a writ of error. They claimed the case was between a state—Georgia— and a foreign nation—the Cherokee—so Georgia had no jurisdiction (authority) in the matter. They asked that Corn Tassel be turned over to the Cherokee legal system.

Georgia Responds

The Supreme Court required Georgia to respond by the second Monday in January 1831. During an emergency meeting of the lawmakers, the state decided to do nothing at all. The lawmakers said that for the United States Supreme Court to interfere with the administration of criminal laws in Georgia was "a flagrant violation of her [the state's] rights."[20]

The state did not even wait for the Court's decision. On December 24, 1830, Georgia proceeded to execute Corn Tassel. About five hundred Cherokees attended the hanging. Tassel's body was given to the tribe for burial.[21] Although Tassel was gone, the Cherokee people continued their legal battle. They believed that the case of *The Cherokee Nation* v. *The State of Georgia* involved vital principles of law and justice that must be settled.

Arguing for a Decision

On March 5, 1831, the attorney for the Cherokee people argued their case before the Supreme Court. Speaking passionately for his cause, William Wirt said,

> We know that whatever can be properly done for this unfortunate people will be done by this honorable court. Their cause is one that must come home to every honest and feeling heart. They have been true and faithful to us and have a right to expect a corresponding fidelity on our part. . . . We asked them to become civilized and they became so. . . . They fought side by side with our present chief magistrate and received his repeated thanks for their gallantry and bravery.[22]

Wirt concluded that the Cherokee people were indeed an independent and foreign nation as defined by the Constitution. He pointed out that the United States government had always treated them as such. Thus, federal laws should govern the situation, not state laws.

Appealing to the purpose of the American justice system itself, Wirt asked, "What is the value of that government in which the decrees of its courts can be mocked at and defied with impunity? . . . It is no government at all."[23] People must be able to trust in the federal government and the laws and treaties it signed, argued Wirt. He also pointed out that many Americans supported the Cherokee people and would support a ruling in their favor. Wirt said:

> I believe . . . that there is a moral force in the public sentiment of the American community which will, alone, sustain it, and constrain obedience. At all events, let us do our duty, and the people of the United States will take care that others do theirs. If they do not, there is an end of the Government, and the Union is dissolved. For, if the Judiciary is struck from the system, what is there, of any value, that will remain?[24]

Georgia did not send anyone to defend its actions before the Court. Clearly, the state was sending a message that it thought the federal government and therefore the Supreme Court had no power in this matter.

What might Georgia have said had it chosen to appear that day? According to historian Leonard Baker, Georgia "could have argued that it was untenable for the state to have within its borders a large population over which she had no control."[25]

Georgia also could have cited the Treaty of 1802, in which the federal government pledged to extinguish Native American claims to land within the state. They could have noted the decision in the *Johnson* case, a ruling that made them confident the Cherokee people could not win.

Now it was up to the Court. How would it handle this difficult situation, complicated by numerous political conflicts? The early 1800s was an era marked by disagreement about what the Supreme Court should do and how much power it should have. Chief Justice Marshall, who served from 1801 to 1835, had steadily and cautiously carved out a role for the Court. A decision for the Cherokee people might well be ignored by both state officials and the president. All of these considerations, along with the specific concerns of the case, weighed heavily on the Justices as they deliberated the case of *Cherokee Nation* v. *The State of Georgia*.

4

A Long-Awaited Decision

Cherokee leaders were eager to hear what the Supreme Court would say about their case and about Native American rights in general. John Ridge and several other Cherokee leaders had come to Washington to watch the arguments. They remained in the city on the morning of March 18, 1831, as they waited, with others, to hear the Court's decision in *Cherokee Nation* v. *The State of Georgia*.

Decisions

Soon, listeners realized that the Court had refused, with a vote of four to two, to issue a ruling on the case. The Court stated that the Cherokee were not a foreign nation and therefore lacked standing to even bring a case before the Supreme Court. The Court refused to deal with the case at all. So, of course, it did not even deal with the question of whether or not Georgia laws could be enforced within the Cherokee Nation. This meant the ruling of the lower court would stand, with its judgment favoring Georgia.

The six Justices had actually divided into three groups of two, with three different opinions. Among those who said that the Cherokee people were not a foreign nation was Chief Justice Marshall, who read the first opinion, which was the opinion for the Court. Marshall began by summarizing the situation that had led to the case at hand. He said that certain laws passed by the state of Georgia ". . . go directly to annihilate the Cherokees as a political society, and to seize, for the use of Georgia, the lands of the nation, which have been assured to them by the United States. . . ."[1] Expressing support for the Cherokee people, Marshall said they had been "numerous, powerful, and truly independent" but had steadily been controlled by white people, giving up lands they had thought would belong to the tribe forever.[2]

The Chief Justice struck what historians have called a middle ground in his ruling. He explained that the Cherokee people had no legal status as a "foreign nation" and thus could not file a legal action against the state of Georgia. Instead, said Marshall, the Cherokee people were a "domestic dependent nation."[3] The Court defined this as a nation that was not sovereign— free and independent—as defined by Article III of the Constitution.[4]

Marshall acknowledged that the Cherokee people were an independent state with independent members. But he said that did not constitute a foreign state as defined by the Constitution. The Chief Justice said that unique and unusual circumstances marked the relationship between the United States and the tribes.[5] One was the location of Native American land inside the territorial borders of the United States. Furthermore, in another unusual aspect of the Cherokee relationship with the United States government, the Cherokee people had sought protection from the government and agreed that the government could regulate their trade.[6]

Responding to arguments that the Constitution of the United States and the federal government clearly viewed the Native Americans as foreign nations, Marshall noted that in one section of the Constitution, Congress received the power to regulate commerce with "foreign Nations, and among the several States, and with the Indian Tribes."[7] This put Native Americans into a third group, separate from both states and foreign nations.

As Marshall finished speaking, it was clear that the Court did not agree with the Cherokee position that they were a nation, independent of the United States even though they were located within its borders. The Court did not move to protect them from the state laws of Georgia. Marshall said that the Court, being a judicial branch of government, did not have the power over a state legislature to take such action now.

Two other Justices had agreed with Marshall's conclusion. One, Justice William Johnson, wrote a separate opinion in which he viewed the status of Native Americans somewhat differently. With Justice Henry Baldwin, Johnson said the Cherokee people were a conquered people. He wrote that they were now "without land that they can call theirs in the sense of property." Yet, said Johnson, "their right of personal self-government has never been taken from them; and such a form of government may exist though the land occupied be in fact that of another."[8]

Though Justice Baldwin agreed with Marshall's conclusion, he used different reasoning. He claimed that tribes could not be considered as distinct, separate states or political entities.[9]

Two other Justices, Smith Thompson and Joseph Story, dissented (disagreed). Both concluded that the Cherokees *were* a foreign nation, according to the definition of a foreign government that was set forth in the Constitution. Thompson wrote:

> The terms *state* and *nation* . . . imply a body of men, united together, to procure their mutual safety and advantage by means of their union. Such a society has its affairs and interests to manage; it deliberates, and it takes resolutions in common, and thus becomes a moral person, having an understanding and a will peculiar to itself, and is susceptible to obligations and laws. . . . Every nation that governs itself, under what form soever, without any dependence on a foreign power, is a sovereign state.[10]

Applying this standard to the Cherokee people, Thompson said, "[I]t is not perceived how it is possible to escape the conclusion, that they form a sovereign state."[11] After all, Thompson pointed out, the Cherokee people had always been treated as a separate nation by the United States government. They were governed by their own laws and customs. They lived within certain bounded territory over which they claimed authority. The Cherokee people had given up land only through treaties. They had never said they would yield control over the rest or give up their own government.

An Uneasy Compromise?

Why had the Court refused to issue a ruling in this case? Looking back, historians believe the Court had to devise a compromise. They had to acknowledge the

In the case of *Cherokee Nation* v. *The State of Georgia*, Justice Thompson (shown here) took the position that the Cherokee people were a separate sovereign nation, independent from the United States.

political realities of the times. That compromise was expressed in Marshall's phrase "dependent domestic nation." Both Marshall and Thompson agreed that the Cherokee people had the right to govern themselves and to occupy traditional lands.

According to historian Wilcomb E. Washburn, Marshall's opinion had to take into account the "natural rights of the Indians," as well as the speculative rights of the earlier European monarchs, the jurisdictional rights of the new American states, and "the practical economic and political demands of the millions who now populate the continent."[12]

The Court also felt at that time that it should limit its role in righting wrongs against the Cherokee people. Justice Marshall said, "This is not a tribunal which can redress the past or prevent the future."[13]

Reactions

At first glance, the Court's decision not to issue its own ruling may have seemed disappointing. Yet after reading the decision, some Cherokee leaders were optimistic. They found ideas that were favorable to their case, especially Chief Justice Marshall's statement that "the Indians are acknowledged to have an unquestionable right to the lands they occupy until that right shall be extinguished by a voluntary cession to our government."[14] Cherokee leaders also were pleased that Marshall had said the Court viewed the Cherokee Nation "as a distinct political society separated from others, capable of managing its own affairs and governing itself."[15]

In addition, after the Court refused to issue a ruling, Marshall sent a sympathetic letter to the tribe.[16] In letters to friends, Marshall said he was not entirely happy with the Court's handling of the case. According to historian Leonard Baker, Marshall wanted to see more public concern expressed toward the Cherokee people and "to keep the case alive."[17] The Chief Justice also believed that, in making treaties with tribes, the United States government had dealt with the tribes as foreign states.

Marshall's wording in *Cherokee Nation* v. *Georgia* had hinted that the Court might at some other time choose to protect certain rights of the Cherokee people. Supporters reprinted favorable sections of the decision in newspapers. A book discussing the case was distributed in New England and other places where people sympathized with the Cherokee people.

Yet there was cause for worry as well. President Jackson and his supporters saw the Court's lack of a ruling as a victory for their side. During one meeting, Jackson told Cherokee leaders that their lawyers were wasting their money with these kinds of legal actions. He warned, "You can live on the lands of Georgia if you choose, but I cannot interfere with the laws of that state to protect you."[18]

The Supreme Court had let the lower court's ruling stand, and President Jackson would not help the Cherokee people. Georgia could continue to defy federal laws and harass the Cherokee people. According to legal scholar Sidney L. Harring, "Through the passage of special laws aimed only at the Cherokee, there was a direct intent to destroy the political, economic, and social infrastructure of the nation. For example, meetings of the tribal council were forbidden, and any Cherokee who acted as a judge in tribal courts was to be punished as a criminal."[19]

On March 23, 1831, a New England clergyman named George B. Cheever wrote to his brother, "You must pray, Henry, for the poor Indians; their prospects for the redress of their accumulated wrongs is sad and dark, almost desperate. Oh the iniquity of this infernal administration!"[20]

Another Chance

In his opinion, Chief Justice Marshall had said only that the Cherokee people lacked the legal standing to sue in a federal court such as the Supreme Court. However, that did not mean *others*—perhaps white citizens of the United States—might not bring such a case against Georgia.

In less than a year, thirty-three-year-old Samuel Austin Worcester found such an opportunity. Worcester was a white man from Vermont who had been ordained as a minister in 1825. After serving for two years in Tennessee, he moved to New Echota, where he helped set up the *Cherokee Phoenix* newspaper in 1828. Worcester wrote articles for the paper. He urged other Americans to demand that the Cherokee people not be subject to Georgia laws.

Near the end of 1831, Wilson Lumpkin succeeded George Gilmer as governor of Georgia and new laws were passed. One law said that all missionaries or other white persons who lived within Cherokee country must obtain a license. These people were also required to take an oath to support and defend the constitution and laws of Georgia. Specifically, the law said:

> [A]ll white persons residing within the limits of the Cherokee nation on the 1st day of March next, or at any time thereafter, without a license or permit from his excellency, the governor, or from such agent as his excellency the governor shall authorize to grant such permit or license, and who shall not have taken the oath hereinafter required, shall be guilty of a high misdemeanor, and, upon conviction, thereof, shall be punished by confinement to the penitentiary, at hard labor, for a term not less than four years.[21]

One reason for this law was to penalize whites who were publicly supporting the Cherokee people. Yet, in an article for the *Phoenix*, Worcester wrote that it was "out of the question" for him to obtain the special license and take the oath of allegiance to the state. He said that taking such oaths would be like conceding that the state had legal power over the Cherokee people.[22]

Worcester received support from his missionary board, of which Jeremiah Evarts was one of the governing members. In January 1832, Worcester told Evarts that he planned to defy the law and remain among the Cherokees without obtaining a state license.[23] Evarts agreed and said that Worcester could count on public support, and perhaps the Supreme Court, if it reached that point. Worcester told his fellow missionaries that he thought they could ultimately rely on the Court. He believed John Marshall's opinion in *Cherokee Nation* v. *The State of Georgia* implied sympathy for the Cherokee position.

Arrested

In March 1832, members of the Georgia Guard arrested Worcester and ten other missionaries they found in Cherokee territory. At the time of his arrest, Worcester had been preaching and translating the Christian Bible into the Cherokee language. He had the permission of the Cherokee leaders to do this. Nine of the missionaries who were arrested agreed to leave the state or to take the required loyalty oath. Worcester and Elizur Butler, another minister, refused. Worcester said that taking the oath "would essentially affect my usefulness as a Missionary laborer among the Cherokees."[24]

On the way to the jail, the men were treated harshly. Butler had to wear a padlock around his neck and was chained to the neck of the horse on which he and his guard were riding. At one point, Butler was injured when the horse stumbled and fell.[25]

Worcester and Butler were tried and convicted of living in the Cherokee nation without permission from the state and for serving as missionaries without a license. After the superior court in Gwinnett County, Georgia, convicted the men, state appellate courts upheld the verdict. Worcester and Butler began serving their sentence—four years of hard labor in the Georgia State Penitentiary at Milledgeville, where they would become model prisoners.

Again, the state was asserting the right to force its laws on the Cherokee people. Once again, the Cherokee people strongly disagreed. The Board of Commissioners for Foreign Missions asked President Jackson to help by asking Georgia to release Worcester

Daniel Webster was one of the Cherokee people's main supporters within the United States government. After the arrest of Samuel Worcester, Webster was one of the officials who continued to support the missionaries.

and Butler. Jackson replied that he had no power to interfere with the laws of a state.[26]

Worcester did have supporters within the government, however. Daniel Webster, Henry Clay, Davy Crockett, Sam Houston, and Theodore Frelinghuysen were among the prominent officials who had long supported the Cherokee cause and now defended the missionaries.

People from Georgia generally sided with the missionaries. They urged Worcester and Butler, however, to ask Governor Lumpkin for a pardon and to accept the state laws. The two prisoners received many visitors, including Dr. Alonzo Church, president of Franklin College, and John MacPherson Berrien, a former United States attorney general. Worcester told them that he hoped his case would reach the Supreme Court. Church and Berrien warned him that bloody confrontations might result if the Supreme Court ordered Georgia to release them.

A New Case in Court

At Worcester's request, William Wirt and John Sergeant again agreed to represent the men in their appeal to the Supreme Court. Wirt told Worcester that their side would probably win but that a decision favoring the Cherokees' rights might not be honored by Georgia officials. He wrote, "It is for yourself alone to consider whether you choose to become the victim by whose suffering this question is to be raised."[27]

Nonetheless, Worcester and Cherokee leaders agreed that the Supreme Court should hear this case. It involved vital matters concerning Native American rights that the Court must address. As he had done before, William Wirt prepared to argue the Cherokee position. He and Sergeant were joined by a third attorney, Elishu Chester, who had represented Worcester and Butler in the court trial.

This time, the Supreme Court agreed to hear the case, which was called *Worcester* v. *Georgia*. On November 10, 1831, Justice Henry Baldwin sent Governor Wilson Lumpkin the official legal notice that arguments for both sides would be heard during the coming term.

Lumpkin told the Georgia General Assembly that he would ignore the case. He said the federal government had never been given "such control over our criminal jurisdiction . . ."[28] Lumpkin vowed to "protect and defend the rights of the state, and use the means afforded to me, to maintain its laws and constitution."[29]

Lumpkin may have felt sure that the Court would not rule against Georgia. When the case was argued

On November 10, 1831, Justice Henry Baldwin (shown here) sent an official notice to Governor Wilson Lumpkin, telling him that the Court would hear *Worchester* v. *Georgia*.

before the Court on February 20, 1832, the state of Georgia did not send anyone to present its side, and did not submit any written arguments. Again, the state ignored the proceedings. William Wirt appeared to plead the case of Samuel Worcester.

In *Cherokee Nation* v. *Georgia*, Wirt had fought to have the Court declare that the Cherokee people were a foreign, sovereign nation under the Constitution. Such a ruling would have entitled them to be heard by the highest court in the land. This time, however, there was no doubt that the Court would issue a ruling on the case. An individual United States citizen was bringing it.

Wirt outlined the facts, explaining that the Reverend Samuel Worcester had lived in the Cherokee Nation for several years. Worcester claimed that as a resident of Cherokee territory, he was outside the jurisdiction of Georgia and was, therefore, subject only to Cherokee laws.

In briefs—formal written arguments—submitted to the Court before oral arguments, Worcester's attorneys claimed that state laws (in this case, those of Georgia) violated treaties made between nations, specifically the Cherokee Nation and the United States government. Under those treaties, Worcester was entitled to stay in the tribe's territory without following Georgia laws. In fact, said Wirt, laws made by Georgia and applied to the Cherokee people were unconstitutional, because they conflicted with the treaties and laws of the United States. Using these arguments, Wirt was asking the Court to deal with the sticky issues of federal versus state powers.

Wirt further pointed out the many instances in which the state of Georgia itself had treated the Cherokee people as a distinct political entity. For example, in 1802, the Georgia Congress had passed a law called a contract of cession in which the Cherokee people were regarded as a nation that could retain its lands unless they gave them up through a legal agreement. It was not until 1828 that the state had begun to abandon that viewpoint and reject the idea of a sovereign Cherokee nation.

Another Tense Wait

Once again, the Cherokee people had gone through the legal process and placed their trust in the Supreme Court. Would the Court disappoint them as it had the previous year? In the two weeks that the Court was deliberating, several Cherokee leaders toured northern states and spoke to the public in order to raise hundreds of dollars for their cause. Thousands of northerners signed a petition that the Cherokees would later present to Congress.

Meanwhile, the Court examined their case. Although most Cherokees did not know it, John Marshall was not the only Justice who resented the way the Cherokee people in Georgia were being treated. Early in 1832, Justice Joseph Story had met some Cherokee leaders in Philadelphia and was impressed by their eloquence and knowledge of the law. In a letter to his wife, Story wrote:

> And I feel, as an American, disgraced by our gross violation of the public faith towards them. I feel, and greatly fear, that in the course of Providence there will be dealt to us a heavy retributive justice. . . .[30]

Would Marshall, Story, and perhaps some other Justices find the courage and legal grounds to rule in the Cherokees' favor this time? In the previous case, the Court had avoided a confrontation with Georgia. It had reached no clear conclusions about the status of Native American tribes or their sovereignty in relation to a state. It had not ruled on the constitutionality of the Georgia laws that now oppressed the Native Americans within the state's borders nor forced President Jackson to take sides with either the state or the Cherokee Nation. What would it do now?

Once again, the Cherokee Nation eagerly waited to hear from the Supreme Court. The tribe's entire future might rest in the hands of these seven men.

5

A Landmark Decision

People packed the courtroom on March 3, 1832, to hear the Court's opinion in *Worcester* v. *Georgia*. The Court reached a decision just two weeks after hearing arguments in the case. Among the spectators that day were several Cherokee leaders and their attorneys, members of Congress, reporters, and members of the public.

Chief Justice Marshall read the majority opinion, in which he was joined by Justices Duvall, Story, and Thompson. At once, he stressed the importance of the case. Speaking in his usual soft voice, the seventy-six-year-old Marshall began, "This cause, in every point of view in which it can be placed, is of the deepest interest."[1] The case, said Marshall, called into question the "validity of the treaties made by the United States with Cherokee Indians. . . ."[2]

"Repugnant to the Constitution"

Marshall went on to explain the circumstances of the case and the laws that had resulted in Samuel Worcester's arrest and conviction.

The first question the Court must answer, said Marshall, was whether or not Georgia had the right to make laws affecting the Cherokee people. Georgia had asserted authority over the Native Americans by requiring missionaries to obtain licenses and take loyalty oaths, then giving the Georgia Guard the power to arrest people who violated these laws. In order to answer this question, the Supreme Court looked at the history of America and its native peoples. Marshall questioned the doctrine of discovery, saying:

> America, separated from Europe by a wide ocean, was inhabited by a distinct people, divided into separate nations, independent of each other and the rest of the world, having institutions of their own, and governing themselves by their own laws. It is difficult to comprehend the [idea], that the inhabitants of either quarter of the globe could have rightful original claims over the inhabitants of the other, or over the lands they occupied; or that the discovery of either by the other should give the discoverer rights in the country discovered, which annulled the pre-existing right of its ancient possessors. . . .[3]

By calling the Native American nations "distinct" and "independent" political communities, Marshall was recognizing that Native Americans living on the continent were not one large group. They were distinct peoples living in separate nations, with the word nation meaning "a people distinct from others."[4]

How did the Justices make this conclusion fit with their conclusions the previous year in *Cherokee Nation v. Georgia*? In that case, Marshall had said that the Cherokee Nation was a dependent one, not a sovereign power. In *Worcester*, Marshall said they were dependent—dependent on the federal government, but not on any state. He reasoned that as distinct, independent political communities, the Native American nations "retain their original natural rights, as the undisputed possessors of the soil, from time immemorial. . . ."[5]

As for the Cherokee Nation, Chief Justice Marshall declared it was a "distinct community, occupying its own territory, with boundaries accurately described, in which the laws of Georgia have no force, and which the citizens of Georgia can have no right to enter, but with the consent of the Cherokees themselves, or in conformity with treaties, and with the acts of Congress."[6]

Discussing the concept of "conquest," Marshall did not dispute the idea that one group of people could conquer another. He said that "power, war, conquest, give rights, which after possession, are conceded by the world. . . ."[7] But the Chief Justice said that conquest did not necessarily give white people the right to govern Native Americans. He pointed out that after arriving in America and in the years since, whites had not taken charge of Native American affairs.

Numerous treaties between the Cherokee people and the United States had been concluded over the years, said Marshall. They clearly laid out the boundary between Cherokee country and the state of Georgia. Therefore, in the Court's opinion, Worcester and others whom the Cherokee invited or permitted to come to their lands were doing so with the permission of the president of the United States and in keeping with federal laws. The government had a duty to protect them when they relied upon those laws.

By now, spectators sensed that Marshall was about to strike down the Georgia law. Speaking in forceful terms, the Chief Justice called the actions of Georgia "repugnant to the Constitution, laws, and treaties of the United States."[8] He said:

> They interfere forcibly with the relations established between the United States and the Cherokee nation, the regulation of which, according to our Constitution, are committed exclusively to the government of the Union. They are in direct hostility with treaties [which] . . . solemnly pledge the faith of

the United States to restrain their citizens from trespassing on [Cherokee lands].[9]

Thus, Marshall declared, the Georgia law must "be reversed and annulled," because it was unconstitutional.[10] The Cherokee people had won. By a vote of four to two (with two Justices, Baldwin and McLean, dissenting and the Justice Johnson away from the Court, ill), the highest court in America had decreed that Georgia could not pass laws affecting the Cherokee people or their land.

Interpreting the Decision

Looking back at the *Worcester* decision, historian Theda Perdue interprets it as one that gave Native Americans "retained sovereignty." She calls this "the idea that a nation retains all those attributes of sovereignty it does not voluntarily surrender."[11] Using Marshall's reasoning, a tribe came to a treaty table with full sovereignty. It could then give up certain specific aspects of its sovereignty in exchange for particular benefits, but still keep all the rights and powers it did not agree to surrender.

In *Worcester*, the Supreme Court was also upholding the right of the federal government to make treaties with foreign nations, without interference by the states. Article VI of the Constitution of the United States

In March 1832, Minister Samuel Worcester (shown here) was arrested for violating a state law that said that all white people living in the Cherokee territory had to obtain a special license from the governor. His case reached the Supreme Court where the law was found to be unconstitutional.

provides that a treaty between the federal government and a foreign nation is supreme, a commitment no state could erase. Marshall said the *Worcester* case brought into question "the validity of treaties made by the United States with the Cherokee Indians. . . ."[12] By making treaties with the Cherokee people through the years, the United States had recognized their sovereignty and their right to the lands they possessed and occupied.

The *Worcester* decision had required courage on the part of the Justices of the Supreme Court. Afterward, Justice Story commented that the Court "had done its duty," saying, "Thanks be to God, the court can wash their hands clean of the iniquity of oppressing the Indians and disregarding their rights."[13]

A Hollow Victory

Among the Cherokee people and their supporters, there was joyful feasting and dancing after news of the *Worcester* decision reached them. One member of the tribe said that the case had forever resolved the question of "who is right and who is wrong."[14]

The Court's ruling meant that the case was remanded (sent back) to the Georgia Supreme Court to be reversed. On March 5, the Court formally ordered Georgia to comply with its ruling. Shortly after that, the Court went into its yearly recess. This meant that if Georgia ignored the order, the state Supreme Court would not be available to take further action until January 1833.

As some people had feared, Georgia did ignore the ruling. The state still refused to release Worcester and Butler from prison or to strike down the laws it had passed against the Cherokee people. Georgia maintained that the United States Supreme Court had no power over state courts or state laws. The state disagreed with the idea that the Court could review or reverse decisions made by its own courts. In his annual message to the state that November, Georgia Governor Lumpkin openly criticized the Supreme Court, referring to the "fallibility, infirmities, and errors of this Supreme tribunal."[15]

Georgia was not the only state to hold this view during those years. Several state governments promoted nullification—ignoring and refuting—any Supreme Court decisions that went against them. Many white Americans feared and disliked Native Americans. Georgia had little to fear by disregarding the Court's orders in *Worcester*.

The Cherokee people were further discouraged when Andrew Jackson won reelection in 1832. As many had expected, President Jackson did not enforce the

Worcester decision or protect the Cherokee people against actions by the state of Georgia. Writing to Worcester after the decision, William Wirt had said that he thought Jackson would do his duty and make Georgia comply, but he was not certain this would happen.

In the years that followed the case, it was reported that Jackson said, "John Marshall has made his decision. Now let *him* enforce it."[16] Some historians think Horace Greeley, a New York journalist, attributed these words to Jackson years after the case was over.[17] But historians do agree that these words reflected Jackson's attitude and behavior.

The two imprisoned missionaries finally gave up in January 1833. They realized that the state did not plan to comply with the Court's ruling. So, Samuel Worcester and Elizur Butler eventually asked Governor Lumpkin for a pardon.

Defying the Federal Government

As the missionaries waited in prison, their fate unresolved, other states took bold actions. The people of South Carolina had watched Georgia defy the Supreme Court. They had seen President Jackson and the rest of the federal government ignore the *Worcester* decision. Now, South Carolina announced that it would not pay federal tariffs or be subject to any Supreme Court decisions. In November 1832, the state passed its Nullification Ordinance. It said that a state could disregard or revoke (nullify) a federal law or ruling it considered unconstitutional.

To their surprise, President Jackson firmly rejected this idea. The president called the nullification law "treason."[18] If necessary, said Jackson, he would call up an army of two hundred thousand men to enforce federal laws. This meant that the President was siding with the Supreme Court's decision that the federal government had legal authority and power over individual states. Jackson urged Congress to pass the Force Bill. This increased the power of the federal government to make states comply with federal laws and taxes.

Jackson might be forced to support the decision in *Worcester*, too. So Governor Lumpkin pardoned Worcester and Butler. This allowed Georgia to avoid a crisis as far as that one case was concerned while still rejecting Cherokee sovereignty.

Escalating Conflicts

Some areas of disagreement between the states and the federal government had now been settled, at least for the moment. But the Cherokee people were still caught in the middle as their problems mounted.

Other Native Americans were affected, too, as states ignored the Worcester decision. Instead, state courts used the ruling in the earlier case of *The State of Georgia v. George Tassels* to justify their actions toward Native Americans within their borders. Historians think that during the 1800s, thousands of Native Americans were tried and convicted of crimes in state courts, then imprisoned or executed.[19] These cases received little publicity. Nor could the defendants afford the expert legal help the Cherokee people had obtained in fighting for their rights.

Despite the *Worcester* case, Georgia passed more laws that threatened the Cherokee people and their property. The Georgia Guard continued to patrol Cherokee lands and arrest Native Americans for various reasons. By the 1830s, there were prominent Cherokee businessmen and plantation owners. They had property of great value, including valuable improvements such as buildings, furnishings, tools, and crops, that Georgia politicians wanted. Politicians in Georgia looked for laws and other ways in which Cherokee property could be taken over by the state.

The case of Joseph Vann, a Cherokee who had fought with Jackson's troops during the Creek War, enraged the tribe. Vann was a wealthy plantation owner whose estate included a brick home, kitchens, outbuildings, mills, fine gardens, fruit orchards, and hundreds of cultivated acres. In 1833, before leaving on a trip, Vann agreed to hire a white man who was applying for a job on his property. When Vann returned home in December, he learned that a new Georgia law banned Cherokees from hiring white workers. A state agent charged Vann with violating the law and declared that the state could now seize his plantation.

During the fight that later took place on Vann's estate, white officials argued over who would get which parts of the property. Gunfire was exchanged, and the house was set on fire. The Vann family had to flee despite the harsh winter weather.

Observing these events, John Marshall was among those who feared that the Cherokee people would be forced not only off of their land, but even out of their homes. On September 22, 1832, Marshall wrote to Justice Joseph Story, "I yield slowly and reluctantly to the conviction that our [C]onstitution cannot last."[20]

Losing Hope

It became clear that the federal government would not stop Georgia from harassing the Cherokee people. State and federal officials expressed little concern about the morality or legality of forcing the Native Americans off their lands and relocating them west of the Mississippi River. According to historian Peter Nabokov:

> The President (whom the Indians had named "Sharp Knife") had both the power to select the tribes that were to be removed and the money—half a million dollars—to finance the giant exodus. To present an illusion of tribal consent, Jackson's secret agents bribed, deceived, and intimidated individual Indians, falsified records, squelched open debate, and finally persuaded some tribesmen to sign in favor of removal.[21]

In December 1835, United States government representatives met with one hundred Cherokees to discuss relocation. They persuaded this group to sign the Treaty of New Echota. It granted all Cherokee lands in the Southeast to the United States in exchange for land in present-day Oklahoma.

Most other Cherokees did not know about this treaty until it was completed. Once they found out about it, however, they disagreed strongly with its terms. Enraged, some fifteen thousand Cherokees signed petitions opposing the Treaty of New Echota. They sent these petitions to Congress, but they got no response. The government insisted that the tribe must leave within two years. All except those who had actually signed the treaty refused to move.

Meanwhile, Georgia continued to insist that it owned all the land within its borders. A land lottery was set up by Georgia lawmakers in 1830. After this, whites clamored to move onto Cherokee land.

Some white settlers feared the Native Americans. In her memoirs, Zillah Haynie Brandon said that when Cherokee men living near her family's homestead drank too much alcohol (supplied by whites), they became "cruel." However, Cherokees and white settlers often lived together peacefully, and some became friends. Brandon also wrote that when the Cherokees had to leave Georgia, white families expressed regret, and gifts were exchanged.[22]

Cherokee supporters in Congress, including Daniel Webster, Henry Clay, and John Calhoun, bitterly attacked the Treaty of New Echota.[23] In March 1838, President Martin Van Buren asked the governors of southeastern states to allow the Cherokee people two more years to leave. The governors refused. George Gilmer, once again the governor of Georgia, said that if the federal government did not remove the Cherokees, he would order state troops to do so.

Led by Principal Chief John Ross, those Cherokees who opposed removal continued to resist. Ross said, "Possessions acquired by unjust and unrighteous means will sooner or later prove a curse to those who sought them."[24]

6

Surviving the Trail of Tears

The Cherokee people now joined other tribes that had been forced to leave the Southeast. The Choctaw, the first of the Five Tribes to be removed, had left in 1831. This was the year the Cherokee people had first appealed to the Supreme Court. The Choctaw had gone to Oklahoma Territory during a severely cold winter. Some Choctaw drowned when an overloaded steamboat sank during the trip; others died of various diseases. Thousands more died within a few years after they arrived. By 1834, the Chickasaw had also been removed to the West, as had the Creek.

Army General Winfield Scott was placed in charge of the Cherokee removal. On May 10, 1838, he told the tribe they must be ready to go within one month. Thousands of Cherokees refused to leave voluntarily, so troops came to oust them at gunpoint. Conflicts erupted, and United States soldiers imprisoned some Cherokees in crowded stockades where cholera and whooping cough, both serious contagious diseases, were rampant. Soldiers set fire to Cherokee villages, farms, and fields.

The Cherokees were outnumbered and had no weapons to fight armed soldiers. Most of them finally agreed to leave. In later years, Rebecca Nuegin, a child during the removal, recalled what happened:

> When the soldiers came to our house, my father wanted to fight, but my mother told him the soldiers would kill him if he did, and we surrendered without a fight. They drove us out of the house to join other prisoners in a stockade.[1]

As they prepared to leave, some Cherokee men showed soldiers medals they had received from Andrew Jackson after the Battle of Horseshoe Bend. Junaluska, the former chief who had once saved Jackson's life, took one last look at the land of his ancestors. He said bitterly, "If I had known Jackson would drive us from our homes, I would have killed him that day at the Horseshoe."[2]

The first group was crowded into boats that headed toward the Tennessee and Mississippi rivers. The remaining thirteen thousand left during the rainy autumn of 1838. With them was their friend Elizur Butler, the missionary who had been imprisoned with Samuel Worcester. The group would endure months of freezing weather and snowstorms before reaching Indian Territory the next March.

A Trail of Tears

The Cherokee journey covered eight hundred miles and became known as the Trail of Tears. The weather was harsh, and the Native Americans ran out of food, clothing, blankets, and medicines during the trip. There were only enough wagons to hold the sick, old, or very young. The majority of Cherokees had to walk most of the way.

Historians believe that about 10 percent of the Cherokee people died during the removal.[3] To the grieving Cherokees, their dead, whom they were not allowed to stop and bury, were like teardrops falling onto the frozen ground; hence the name Trail of Tears.

Principal Chief John Ross's wife was among those who did not survive. During a snowstorm, Quatie Ross, who was already ill, gave her blanket to a sick child, leaving herself vulnerable to the cold winds. Within days, Quatie Ross died of pneumonia. Thousands more Cherokees from this group would also die within a few years of reaching the West.

Principal Chief John Ross led the group of Cherokees who opposed the relocation forced upon them after they signed the Treaty of New Echota.

Back East, journalists exposed the grim realities of the Cherokee removal. Travelers and soldiers who had witnessed the events described the suffering of the Cherokee people and the high number of deaths. Many Americans were outraged. In the Senate, Daniel Webster criticized federal policies, saying, "There is a strong and growing feeling that a great wrong has been done to the Cherokee."[4]

A Disunited People

In March 1839, the surviving Cherokees reached Oklahoma Territory. It was a drier, hotter place than their former homelands, but this is where they started over. These Cherokees were called members of the National Party. Living there already were members of the Treaty Party, led by Stand Watie and John Ridge. A third group of Cherokees, who had settled in Arkansas years before, were also sent to join them in Oklahoma. The Arkansas Cherokees were called the Old Settlers.

Conflicts among the groups intensified after John Ross and his group arrived. The survivors of the Trail of Tears were still hostile toward those who had signed the Treaty of New Echota. Some quarrels exploded into violence. On June 22, Treaty Party leader John Ridge and two other party members were murdered. By signing away Cherokee land, they were guilty of treason in the eyes of some Cherokees. Stand Watie, one of the intended victims, managed to escape. He and his supporters began plotting revenge. The divided factions of Cherokees seemed headed toward disaster.

Urging unity, National Party leader John Ross asked people to set aside their grievances and reason with each other. The men who had killed the Treaty Party leaders were pardoned. In 1839, Ross was reelected as principal chief. The groups reorganized themselves as the United Cherokee, under a new constitution. It said that all Cherokees in the West belonged to the same tribe, ruled by one government. They pledged to live in peace with other Native Americans and with whites. At the same time, the Cherokee people intended to "peaceably seek . . . redress from the scales of justice upheld by the United States."[5]

Nonetheless, fights often broke out during the next seven years. In 1846, Ross, Watie, and the other leaders reached a new agreement. The Cherokee people worked together to rebuild their nation.

Rebuilding Institutions

Through hard work and resourcefulness, the Cherokee people managed to succeed against the odds and eventually prosper in the West. From their capital, in Tahlequah, Oklahoma, they set up courts and a

In the summer of 1838, the United States government began to forcibly remove all remaining Cherokees from Georgia. After marching along the Trail of Tears those who survived were forced to relocate to Oklahoma.

legislature, as well as a fine educational system. The school system, serving both men and women, was remarkable for its time.

Farming was difficult in Oklahoma Territory, but a number of Cherokees managed to raise crops. Many Cherokees also became ranchers and salt merchants, like their white neighbors. Some Native Americans became wealthy plantation owners with slaves to work in their fields. Other Cherokees opposed slavery. This sparked debates that also raged among white Americans during this era.

The tribe still believed in the principles they had championed during their Supreme Court cases—that they were a sovereign nation entitled to self-rule. The first issue of their new newspaper, the *Cherokee Advocate*, was published in 1844 with the motto "Our Rights—Our Country—Our Race." It was a brave statement of the Cherokee philosophy. The nation intended to endure.

Civil War

In 1861, conflicts over slavery and other matters splintered the United States into North and South and the Civil War began. Many Cherokees supported the slave-owning South, called the Confederacy. Arguments divided Cherokees who supported the Union, as the antislavery North was known, and those who favored the Confederacy. After Principal Chief John Ross switched his loyalty to the North near the end of the war, some Cherokees joined him.

The United States government resented Cherokees who had supported the Confederacy, especially those who had joined its army. In 1862, Congress urged President Abraham Lincoln to cancel all treaties then in existence with the tribe. New treaties were negotiated, leaving the Cherokee people with even less land.

The North finally won the war, which ended on April 9, 1865. After the war, more settlers poured into the West, including into Cherokee lands. Outlaws from other regions also settled among them since Native American laws did not apply to whites.

The United States government made plans to connect the east and west coasts by railroad. It enacted a new treaty that allowed the government to build rail lines through Cherokee territory. This treaty also required the Cherokee people to give up their slaves and let Delaware and Shawnee Indians from the Midwest share Cherokee land in Oklahoma.

During these negotiations, John Ross fought to maintain Cherokee rights that had been granted under previous treaties. It was a fight Ross pursued until he died at age seventy-six, in 1866.

Another Legal Struggle

During the 1860s, the federal government negotiated its last series of treaties with Native Americans. The United States now had authority over millions of acres allocated as "Indian reservations." In 1871, Congress passed a law banning further treaties between different tribes and the federal government. This ended the idea of any nation-to-nation relationships, with the United States and the Cherokee Nation regarding each other as equals.

In 1883, another major case involving Native American rights reached the United States Supreme Court. It had been fifty years since the Cherokee people had fought their famous legal battles. During that time, the Court had heard some twenty cases involving Native Americans, but none raised such major issues as the Cherokee Cases had. The Court had not formed a clear or consistent policy toward Native Americans. Native American rights continued to be attacked by individuals, states, and the federal government.

The 1883 Supreme Court case developed after Crow Dog, a Brulé Sioux, killed a Sioux leader named Spotted Tail on the Sioux reservation in the summer of 1881. South Dakota officials said that Crow Dog should be tried in state courts, not those of the reservation. Crow Dog was arrested, convicted of murder in the South Dakota court, then sentenced to death. Yet, among the Sioux, his crime was regarded as an execution, not a murder. This called for a different penalty than being put to death.

The United States Supreme Court was asked to rule on whether or not federal courts had authority (jurisdiction) over crimes committed on Native American lands. Declaring that state and federal courts did not have such authority to convict people, the Supreme Court pardoned Crow Dog. Congress then created an exception to the Court's ruling by passing the Major Crimes Act of 1884. Under the act, Native Americans who committed a major crime, such as murder, against another Native American were subject to the laws of the state or territory in which the crime occurred.

More Broken Promises

By the 1880s, Native Americans were adjusting to increasing white settlement in the West. New difficulties arose, however. More tribes were assigned to live on specified lands called reservations. To compensate for their losses, the United States government gave them cash and material goods—but often less than had been promised by treaty.

In 1887, Senator Henry Dawes of Massachusetts sponsored the controversial General Allotment Act, also

In 1883, another case involving Native American rights reached the Supreme Court. Crow Dog (above) had committed a murder on the Sioux reservation, and it was unclear whether or not the state of South Dakota had the right to try him in its courts.

known as the Dawes Act. The act divided up reservation lands and gave out plots to individual Native Americans. The land that remained, about 90 million acres, went to the United States government and was offered for sale.

In 1888, leaders of the Cherokee, Choctaw, Creek, Chickasaw, and Seminole tribes met with officials from the Bureau of Indian Affairs at Fort Gibson, Oklahoma. They were there to protest the Dawes Act. When the Cherokee people were removed to the West fifty years earlier, the United States government had signed an agreement promising they would never again be forced to move. All of the tribes had received legal titles to their lands. This meant that they alone had authority over it. They were certain they could not be subject to the Dawes Act and were exempted from it in the beginning.

But as other reservations were being created and white homesteaders crowded the region, the federal government was pressed to sell Cherokee lands, too. Many whites also thought the Native Americans should be assimilated—should become part of mainstream white culture—and would be better off without tribal affiliations.

In 1893, Congress dissolved the tribal governments. The Dawes Commission visited Oklahoma and allowed whites to testify before Congress about the need to divide up Cherokee lands. In 1895, Congress approved a survey of those lands. Three years later, in 1898, it passed the Curtis Act, which would divide up those lands for sale. Independent Native American school systems were terminated and put under the direction of the Bureau of Indian Affairs.

After individual Native Americans received parcels of land, whites often urged them to sell those, too. Some dishonest people cheated some Native Americans out of all of their property.

Many of the Cherokees refused to sign papers accepting land allotments, but they were forced to do so. In 1906, seventy-six-year-old DeWitt Clinton Duncan, a Cherokee, told a Senate committee about the devastating problems the land divisions had caused. Duncan was a graduate of Dartmouth College. He had once farmed three hundred acres of land, but the government took away all but sixty acres. His land was taken just as the corn crop was ripening. Duncan called this an "outrage," and said:

> For the last few years, since I have had my allotment, I have gone out there on that farm day after day. I have used the ax, the hoe, the spade, the plow, hour for hour, until fatigue would throw me exhausted upon the ground. . . . I have exerted all my ability, all industry . . . my will, my ambition, the love of my wife . . . to make my living out of that 60 acres, and,

God be my judge, I have not been able to do it. I am
not able to do it. I can't do it. I have not been able to
clear expenses. . . . [W]hen I use the word "I" I mean
the whole Cherokee people. . . . What am I to do?[6]

That same year, Native Americans throughout
America were subjected to more changing policies and
dislocations. The tribes in Oklahoma were told that
their governments and tribal court systems had been
terminated. Their leaders no longer had any authority.

Fighting for Their Rights

With the 1900s came more shifting policies. In 1924,
Congress passed a law making Native Americans eligi-
ble for United States citizenship. The Indian
Reorganization Act (IRA) was passed in 1936. The act
ended land divisions and budgeted $2 million a year for
the federal government to buy land that would then be
returned to Native Americans. The IRA allowed tribal
governments some self-government. They were, however, subject to the approval of the Secretary of the
Interior. Groups on the reservations could vote on a
constitution and bylaws.

For the Cherokee people and other groups, it was a
time of decisions. Should they stop asserting their rights
under treaties made through the years in the wake of
this new government plan? Would becoming United

States citizens, with the rights that implied, force them to lose any hope of sovereignty?

After World War II (1939–45), the Supreme Court decision in *Worcester* v. *Georgia*, now more than a century old, gained new importance. Judges, public officials, and Native American leaders began citing Marshall's opinion in support of Indian sovereignty. One of Marshall's key points—that a nation does not lose those aspects of sovereignty that it does not give up voluntarily—was repeated numerous times after the 1940s.

A new mood swept across America during the 1950s and 1960s. More and more, the victims of legal and social injustices began speaking out and demanding equal rights. A civil rights movement led by African Americans inspired similar movements by women, Native Americans, and others.

For Native Americans, the survival of their communities and tribal rights was as much a part of the struggle as was gaining rights as individuals. Most tribes at that time lived on lands that were now only a fraction of the size of their original ancestral lands, while others, such as the Cherokee people, had been moved. Native American historian Vine Deloria, Jr., a Sioux says, "The tribes were concerned about their separate existence as dependent nations for whom the

United States had a responsibility . . . that the original status of Indians be respected."[7]

In 1963, several Native Americans joined a civil rights demonstration called the March on Washington, but there were no large Indian delegations present. In the years that followed, Native Americans held their own demonstrations. One was a 1964 fish-in held in Washington State. It was staged to protest violations of treaties that guaranteed fishing rights to Native Americans in the Pacific Northwest. Actor Marlon Brando and African-American activist Dick Gregory joined the protesters.

Two years later, an important "first" took place in Santa Fe, New Mexico. Native American leaders convinced officials from the Department of the Interior, the federal government agency that included the Bureau of Indian Affairs, to consult with them before developing laws that would have a major impact on tribes throughout the nation. These leaders were also invited to send representatives to a planning meeting being held by the department.

Says Vine Deloria, Jr.,:

> The obvious success of the marches and demonstrations in getting policies changed taught a very important lesson to many young Indians, who had seen their fathers and grandfathers thwarted by the immense bureaucracy of the federal government.[8]

A New Trail

In the 1960s, more than a century after the Cherokee Cases of the 1830s, the Cherokees in the western United States sued the federal government. The lawsuit claimed that the government owed the tribe money for illegally forcing them to sell land in 1893. The United States Supreme Court awarded the tribe $15 million. They used the money to build a cultural center and buy more land for the tribe's use.

After years of having their institutions crushed, the Cherokee people finally regained the right to elect their own leaders and organize a tribal government. In 1970, Congress passed new laws to this effect. Ross Swimmer was elected principal chief of the Cherokee tribe the next year. He was the first person to serve in that position during the 1900s. Another first occurred in 1985 when Wilma Mankiller became the first woman chosen as principal chief of the Cherokee people.

In 1972, one thousand Native Americans gathered in Washington, D.C., to form what they called the Trail of Broken Treaties. The group met with United States officials to discuss problems facing Native Americans. They asked President Richard Nixon to give Native Americans a new status called treaty relations.[9] The government replied that the Indian Citizenship Act of 1924 had made Native Americans individual United

States citizens. Because of this, tribes could no longer be viewed as groups with whom the government could make treaties.

Native American leaders recognized an increasing ability to influence political decisions. They organized and met as a group to plan their activities. The National Congress of American Indians (NCAI) took an active role in reviewing any pending laws that would affect Native Americans. The American Indian Movement (AIM), led by Dennis Banks, organized numerous demonstrations. During and after the 1960s and 1970s, more Native Americans were also returning to the reservations to live or to take part in ceremonies and activities.

The Legacy of the Cherokee Cases

Looking back at the legal struggles of the Cherokee people in the 1830s, historians believe they had a great impact. The decision in *Cherokee Nation* v. *The State of Georgia*, according to Vine Deloria, Jr., "dominated all legal theory concerning American Indians for nearly a century and a half."[10] Unfortunately, it was used to justify mistreating Native Americans, both as individuals and as groups.

It is not possible to know how history would have changed had the 1831 case been decided differently. It is also impossible to know what would have happened

In 1985, Wilma Mankiller became the first woman to be selected as principal chief of the Cherokee people.

if President Jackson had enforced the bold decision the Court made in *Worcester* v. *Georgia*. The Supreme Court was not able to stop the greed and political motivations that worked against the Cherokee people. This eventually led to their removal and the Trail of Tears. In the decades since 1832, critics have continued to condemn Andrew Jackson, the state of Georgia, and others in the United States government for defying the *Worcester* decision. Historian Leonard Baker writes:

> . . . through generations that followed, they came to understand that the morality spoken by the Marshall Court in the decision of *Worcester* v. *Georgia* was a call to the conscience of the American people. Nothing can excuse the ruthlessness of the whites toward the Indians; and the conduct of the state of Georgia, and of Andrew Jackson in refusing to enforce the Court's decision, demonstrates the folly of refusing to obey the law. The people decided, as Jackson had predicted. They had recorded in their histories that Andrew Jackson and the state of Georgia acted to deprive people of their legal rights. In a nation built on law, there can be no greater condemnation.[11]

Questions for Discussion

The Cherokee Cases—and the way in which whites treated Native Americans in general after settling in North and South America—sparked heated debates that continue to this day. The Supreme Court addressed some of those matters in its 1831 and 1832 decisions. The decisions discussed the status of Native Americans and the rights that white Americans might have over Native Americans whom they viewed as "conquered." The Court also carefully concluded that a conquered nation can retain certain aspects of its independence that it does not willingly give up.

Here are some other important questions that arise when looking at these cases and at the troubled history of relations between whites and Native Americans.

1. Many Americans harshly criticized officials in Georgia and the United States government. How did the state and federal governments justify their actions toward the Cherokee people?

2. Did winning the Revolutionary War against England entitle the new United States to the lands the British had claimed, despite the fact that Native Americans were living there?

3. What choices and alternatives were available to the people of Georgia during the early 1800s? Why did they prefer not to adjust to living side by side with the Cherokees, allowing the tribe to exist as a separate nation inside their state borders?

4. Why did the state of Georgia choose not to wait and hope the Cherokee people might someday change their minds and move west of their own accord?

5. What events led Georgians to believe that they would not be penalized for their treatment of the Cherokee people?

6. Why did the United States government keep changing its policies toward Native Americans and break so many promises?

7. The United States government believed that the Cherokee people should be paid for the land they gave up and that their resettlement should be financed by the government. How did the Cherokee people view their offer? Was the settlement a fair one?

Chapter Notes

Chapter 1

1. Address of the "Committee and Council of the Cherokee Nation in General Council Convened to the People of the United States." Reprinted in *Jeremiah Evarts, Cherokee Removal: The "William Penn" Essays and Other Writings*, edited and with an introduction by Francis Paul Prucha (Knoxville, Tenn.: University of Tennessee Press, 1981), p. 254.

2. Ibid, p. 255.

3. Ibid., pp. 254–55.

4. Peter Nabokov, ed., *Native American Testimony: A Chronicle of Indian-White Relations From Prophecy to the Present* (New York: Viking Penguin, 1991), pp. 121–22.

5. Ibid., pp. 122–123.

6. Ibid., p. 123.

7. Ibid.

8. Wilcomb E. Washburn, *Red Man's Land, White Man's Law: A Study of the Past and Present Status of American Indians* (New York: Charles Scribner's Sons, 1971), p. 66.

Chapter 2

1. Theda Perdue and Michael D. Green, *The Cherokee Removal: A Brief History with Documents* (Boston: Bedford Books of St. Martin's Press, 1995), p. 5.

2. Wilcomb E. Washburn, *Red Man's Land, White Man's Law: A Study of the Past and Present Status of American Indians* (New York: Charles Scribner's Sons, 1971), p. 67.

3. Samuel Carter III, *Cherokee Sunset: A Nation Betrayed* (Garden City, N.Y.: Doubleday, 1976), p. 11.

4. Jeremiah Evarts, *Cherokee Removal: The William Penn Essays and Other Writings*, ed. Francis Paul Prucha (Knoxville, Tenn.: University of Tennessee Press, 1981), p. 60.

5. Ibid., pp. 60–61.

6. Carter III, pp. 12–13.

7. Perdue and Green, p. 24.

8. Leonard Baker, *John Marshall: A Life in Law* (New York: Macmillan, 1974), p. 733.

9. Thurman Wilkins, *Cherokee Tragedy: The Story of the Ridge Family and the Decimation of a People* (New York: Macmillan, 1970), p. 141.

10. Perdue and Green, p. 58.

11. Carter, p. 40.

12. Ulrich Bonnell Phillips, "The Expulsion of the Cherokees," Louis Filler and Allen Guttman, eds., *The Removal of the Cherokees: Manifest Destiny or National Dishonor?* (Boston: D.C. Heath, 1962), p. 3.

13. Ibid.

Chapter 3

1. Andrew Jackson, First Inaugural Address, March 4, 1829, quoted in Joseph Burke, "The Cherokee Cases: A Study in Law, Politics, and Morality," *Stanford Law Review*, February 1969, p. 504.

2. Ibid.

3. *Johnson and Graham's Lessee* v. *McIntosh* 8 Wheaton 543 (1823); quoted in Washburn, p. 66.

4. Ibid., pp. 574, 591.

5. Ibid.

6. Wilcomb E. Washburn, *Red Man's Land, White Man's Law: A Study of the Past and Present Status of American Indians* (New York: Charles Scribner's Sons, 1971), p. 67.

7. Leonard Baker, *John Marshall: A Life in Law* (New York: Macmillan, 1974), pp. 731–32.

8. Theda Perdue and Michael D. Green, *The Cherokee Removal: A Brief History with Documents* (Boston: Bedford Books of St. Martin's Press, 1995), p. 116.

9. Ibid., pp. 116–117.

10. Ibid., p. 120.

11. Ibid.

12. Grace Steele Woodward, *The Cherokees* (Norman, Okla.: University of Oklahoma Press, 1963), pp. 158–59; Wilkins, p. 203; Perdue and Green, pp. 63–67.

13. Perdue and Green, p. 68.

14. Jeremiah Evarts, *Speeches on the Passage of the Bill, for the Removal of the Indians, Delivered in the Congress of the United States, April and May, 1830* (Knoxville, Tenn.: University of Tennessee Press), p. 263.

15. Samuel Carter III, *Cherokee Sunset: A Nation Betrayed* (Garden City, N.Y.: Doubleday, 1976), pp. 96–97.

16. Charles Warren, *The Supreme Court in United States History* (Boston: Little Brown, 1937), p. 731.

17. Calvin Colton, *Tour of the American Lakes and Among the Indians of the Northwest in 1830.* London: 1833, pp. 171–72; as quoted in Thurman Wilkins, *Cherokee Tragedy: The Story of the Ridge Family and the Decimation of a People* (New York: Macmillan, 1970), p. 211.

18. John P. Kennedy, *Memoirs of the Life of William Wirt,* Vol. II (Philadelphia: William S. Hein & Company Inc., 1856), p. 255.

19. Ibid., pp. 259–260.

20. Thurman Wilkins, *Cherokee Tragedy: The Story of the Ridge Family and the Decimation of a People* (New York: Macmillan, 1970), p. 209.

21. Sidney L. Harring, *Crow Dog's Case: American Indian Sovereignty, Tribal Law, and United States Law in the Nineteenth Century* (New York: Cambridge University Press, 1994), p. 30.

22. Richard Peters, *The Case of the Cherokee Nation Against the State of Georgia* (Philadelphia: Thomas, Coperthwait, & Co., 1831), pp. 157–58; Wilkins, p. 215.

23. Baker, p. 736.

24. Kennedy, pp. 291–293.

25. Baker, p. 736.

Chapter 4

1. *The Cherokee Nation v. The State of Georgia, Peters Reports* V, 75-20 in Louis Filler and Allen Guttman, eds. *The Removal of the Cherokees: Manifest Destiny or National Dishonor?* (Boston: D.C. Heath, 1962), p. 61.

2. Ibid.

3. Theda Perdue and Michael D. Green, *The Cherokee Removal: A Brief History with Documents* (Boston: Bedford Books of St. Martin's Press, 1995), pp. 68–69.

4. Ibid.

5. Leonard Baker, *John Marshall: A Life in Law* (New York: Macmillan, 1974), p. 738.

6. Ibid.

7. Ibid.

8. *The Cherokee Nation v. The State of Georgia, Peters Reports* V, in Vine Deloria, Jr., *Behind the Trail of Broken Treaties: An Indian Declaration of Independence* (New York: Delacorte Press, 1974), p. 115.

9. *The Cherokee Nation* v. *The State of Georgia*, 304.S.1, pp. 47–48 (1831).

10. Vine Deloria, Jr., *Behind the Trail of Broken Treaties: An Indian Declaration of Independence* (New York: Delacorte Press, 1974), pp. 115–116.

11. Ibid., 117.

12. Wilcomb E. Washburn, *Red Man's Land, White Man's Law* (New York: Charles Scribner's Sons, 1971), p. 66.

13. Robert Shnayerson, *The Illustrated History of the Supreme Court of the United States* (New York: Harry N. Abrams, Inc., 1986), p. 99.

14. Samuel Carter III, *Cherokee Sunset: A Nation Betrayed* (Garden City, N.Y.: Doubleday, 1976), p. 113.

15. *The Cherokee Nation* v. *The State of Georgia* 30 U.S. 1831, pp. 16, 17.

16. Thurman Wilkins, *Cherokee Tragedy: The Story of the Ridge Family and of the Decimation of a People* (New York: Macmillan, 1970), p. 217.

17. Baker, p. 740.

18. Letter from John Ridge to Elias Boudinot, published in the *Cherokee Phoenix*, May 21, 1831, quoted in Wilkins, p. 217.

19. Sidney L. Harring, *Crow Dog's Case: American Indian Sovereignty, Tribal Law, and United States Law in the Nineteenth Century* (New York: Cambridge University Press, 1994), p. 32.

20. Jeremiah Evarts, *Cherokee Removal: The "William Penn" Essays and Other Writings*, edited and with an introduction by Francis Paul Prucha (Knoxville, Tenn.: University of Tennessee Press, 1981), p. 38.

21. Perdue and Green, p. 72.

22. Edwin A. Miles, "After John Marshall's Decision: Worcester v. Georgia and the Nullification Crisis," *The Journal of Southern History*, November 1973, p. 2.

23. Ibid., p. 2.

24. Ibid., p. 6.

25. Ibid., p. 6.

26. Ibid., p. 8.

27. Ibid., p. 7.

28. Baker, p. 741.

29. Ibid.

30. Ibid.

Chapter 5

1. *Worcester* v. *Georgia, Peters Reports*, VI, pp. 536–563 in Louis Filler and Allen Guttman, eds. *The Removal of the Cherokees: Manifest Destiny or National Dishonor?* (Boston: D.C. Heath, 1962), p. 69.

2. Theda Perdue and Michael D. Green, *The Cherokee Removal: A Brief History with Documents* (Boston: Bedford Books of St. Martins Press, 1995), p. 71.

3. Ibid., pp. 72–73.

4. Ibid., p. 73.

5. Louis Filler and Allen Guttman, eds. *The Removal of the Cherokees: Manifest Destiny or National Dishonor?* (Boston: D.C. Heath, 1962) p. 75.

6. Ibid., p. 77.

7. Leonard Baker, *John Marshall: A Life in Law* (New York: Macmillan, 1974), p. 743.

8. Filler and Guttman, p. 78.

9. Perdue and Green, pp. 74–75.

10. Ibid., p. 74.

11. Ibid., p. 69.

12. Ibid., p. 71.

13. Letter by Justice Joseph Story to his wife, March 4, 1832, in John F. Dillon, *John Marshall—Life, Character, and Judicial Services* (Chicago: Fred B. Rothman & Company, 1903), p. 681.

14. Edwin A. Miles, "After John Marshall's Decision: Worcester v. Georgia and the Nullification Crisis," *The Journal of Southern History*, November 1973, p. 11.

15. Perdue and Green, p. 69.

16. Archibald Cox, *The Court and the Constitution* (Boston: Houghton Mifflin, 1987) p. 14.

17. Robert Shnayerson, *The Illustrated History of the Supreme Court of the United States* (New York: Harry N. Abrams, Inc., 1986), p. 99.

18. Ibid., p. 101.

19. Sidney L. Harring, *Crow Dog's Case: American Indian Sovereignty, Tribal Law, and United States Law in the Nineteenth Century* (New York: Cambridge University Press, 1994), p. 34.

20. Wilcomb E. Washburn, *Red Man's Land, White Man's Law: A Study of the Past and Present Status of American Indians* (New York: Charles Scribner's Sons, 1971), p. 69

21. Peter Nabokov, ed., *Native American Testimony: A Chronicle of Indian-White Relations From Prophecy to the Present* (New York: Viking Penguin, 1991), pp. 148–49.

22. Perdue and Green, pp. 89–91.

23. Royce, *The Cherokee Nation*, p. 290.

24. Elizabeth West, "The Great Chiefs," *Cobblestone*, February 1984, p. 30.

Chapter 6

1. Peter Nabokov, *Native American Testimony: A Chronicle of Indian-White Relations From Prophecy to the Present* (New York: Viking Penguin, 1991), pp. 149–50.

2. Elizabeth West, "The Great Chiefs," *Cobblestone*, February 1984, p. 29.

3. Francis Paul Prucha, "Doing Indian History," in Smith and Kvasnicka, eds. *Indian White Relations*, p. 6.

4. Ibid.

5. Samuel Carter III, *Cherokee Sunset: A Nation Betrayed* (Garden City, N.Y.: Doubleday, 1976), p. 273.

6. Nabokov, pp. 266–67.

7. Vine Deloria, Jr., *Behind the Trail of Broken Treaties* (New York: Delacorte Press, 1974), p. 24.

8. Ibid., p. 25.

9. Ibid., pp. xi-xii.

10. Ibid., p. 114.

11. Leonard Baker, *John Marshall: A Life in Law* (New York: Macmillan, 1974), p. 746.

Bibliography

Anderson, William L., ed. *Cherokee Removal: Before and After.* Athens, Ga.: University of Georgia Press, 1991.

Baker, Leonard. *John Marshall: A Life in Law.* New York: Macmillan, 1974.

Carter, Samuel, III. *Cherokee Sunset: A Nation Betrayed.* Garden City, N.Y.: Doubleday, 1976.

Corkran, David H. *Cherokee Frontier: Conflict and Survival.* Norman, Okla.: University of Oklahoma Press, 1962.

Cox, Archibald. *The Court and the Constitution.* Boston: Houghton Mifflin, 1987.

Deloria, Vine, Jr. *Behind the Trail of Broken Treaties.* New York: Delacorte Press, 1974.

Edmunds, R. David. *American Indian Leaders.* Lincoln, Nebr.: University of Nebraska Press, 1980.

Ehle, John. *Trail of Tears: The Rise and Fall of the Cherokee Nation.* Garden City, N.Y.: Doubleday, 1988.

Evarts, Jeremiah. *Cherokee Removal: The "William Penn" Essays and Other Writings.* Edited and with an introduction by Francis Paul Prucha. Knoxville, Tenn.: University of Tennessee Press, 1981.

Filler, Louis, and Allen Guttman. *The Removal of the Cherokee Nation: Manifest Destiny or National Dishonor?* Boston: D.C. Heath, 1962.

Foreman, Grant. *Indian Removal: The Emigration of the Five Civilized Tribes of Indians.* Norman, Okla.: University of Oklahoma Press, 1953.

Harring, Sidney L. *Crow Dog's Case: American Indian Sovereignty, Tribal Law, and United States Law in the Nineteenth Century.* New York: Cambridge University Press, 1994.

Johnson, Stephen L. *Guide to American Indian Documents in the Congressional Serials Set, 1817–1899.* New York: Clearwater Publishing Co., 1977.

Lumpkin, Wilson. *The Removal of the Cherokee Indians From Georgia.* New York: Dodd, Mead, 1907.

Malone, Henry Thompson. *Cherokees of the Old South.* Athens, Ga.: University of Georgia Press, 1956.

McLoughlin, William G. *Cherokee Renascence in the New Republic.* Princeton, N.J.: Princeton University Press, 1986.

Moulton, Gary E. *John Ross, Cherokee Chief.* Athens, Ga.: University of Georgia Press, 1978.

————. *The Papers of Chief John Ross.* 2 vols. Norman, Okla.: University of Oklahoma Press, 1985.

Nabokov, Peter, ed. *Native American Testimony: A Chronicle of Indian-White Relations From Prophecy to the Present.* New York: Viking Penguin, 1991.

Nammack, Georgiana C. *Fraud, Politics, and the Dispossession of the Indians.* Norman, Okla.: University of Oklahoma Press, 1969.

Perdue, Theda, and Michael D. Green. *The Cherokee Removal: A Brief History with Documents.* Boston: Bedford Books of St. Martin's Press, 1995.

Perkerson, Medora Field. *White Columns in Georgia.* New York: Crown, 1952.

Peters, Richard, ed. *Report of Cases Argued and Adjudged in the Supreme Court of the United States, January Term, 1832.* Philadelphia: Thomas, Cowperthwait, & Co., 1845.

Phillips, Ulrich B. *Georgia and State Rights*. Washington, D.C.: U.S. Government Printing Office, 1902.

Satz, Ronald N. *American Indian Policy in the Jacksonian Era*. Lincoln, Nebr.: University of Nebraska Press, 1975.

Shnayerson, Robert. *The Illustrated History of the Supreme Court of the United States*. New York: Harry N. Abrams, Inc., 1986.

Smith, Jane F. and Robert M. Kvasnicka. *Indian-White Relations: A Persistent Paradox*. Washington, D.C.: Howard University Press, 1976.

Strickland, Rennard. *Fire and the Spirits: Cherokee Law from Clan to Court*. Norman, Okla.: University of Oklahoma Press, 1975.

Viola, Herman. *Thomas L. McKenney: Architect of America's Early Indian Policy, 1816-1830*. Chicago: Swallow Press, 1974.

Wardell, Morris L. *A Political History of the Cherokee Nation: 1838-1907*. Norman, Okla.: University of Oklahoma Press, 1938.

Warren, Charles. *The Supreme Court in United States History*. Boston: Little, Brown, 1923.

Washburn, Wilcomb E. *Red Man's Land, White Man's Law*. New York: Charles Scribner's Sons, 1971.

Westin, Alan F. *An Autobiography of the Supreme Court*. New York: Macmillan, 1963.

White, G. Edward. *The American Judicial Tradition: Profiles of Leading American Judges*. New York: Oxford University Press, 1976.

Wilbrun, H. C. *Chief Junaliska*. Asheville, N.C.: Stephens Press, 1951.

Wilkins, Thurman. *Cherokee Tragedy: The Story of the Ridge Family and of the Decimation of a People*. New York: Macmillan, 1970.

Wilkinson, Charles F. *American Indians, Time and the Law.* New Haven, Conn.: Yale University Press, 1987.

Woodward, Grace Steele. *The Cherokees.* Norman, Okla.: University of Oklahoma Press, 1963.

Articles

Brown, Dee. "The Trail of Tears." *American History Illustrated.* June 1972 (Vol. VII, No. 3).

Burke, Joseph C. "The Cherokee Cases: A Study in Law, Politics, and Morality." *Stanford Law Review*, February 1969.

Miles, Edwin A. "After John Marshall's Decision: Worcester v. Georgia and the Nullification Crisis." *The Journal of Southern History*, November 1973.

Perdue, Theda. "Cherokee Women and the Trail of Tears." *Journal of Women's History*, January 1989.

West, Elizabeth. "The Great Chiefs." *Cobblestone*, February 1984.

Index